T0197090

Putting People Back in Politics

A Manual for the Disgruntled

Edward Schneier

authorHOUSE®

AuthorHouse™
1663 Liberty Drive
Bloomington, IN 47403
www.authorhouse.com
Phone: 1 (800) 839-8640

Published by AuthorHouse 02/22/2018

ISBN: 978-1-5462-2817-2 (sc)
ISBN: 978-1-5462-2818-9 (e)

Library of Congress Control Number: 2018901654

Print information available on the last page.

Any people depicted in stock imagery provided by Getty Images are models, and such images are being used for illustrative purposes only. Certain stock imagery © Getty Images.

This book is printed on acid-free paper.

Contents

Preface

This my tenth book, the first nine of which were with traditional publishing houses. I chose to self-publish this one because none of the publishers I contacted could produce a book in fewer than six months. Thanks to Authorhouse for being able to do this.

I wrote *Putting People Back in Politics* largely in response to a number of friends and neighbors who asked me— as a student of politics— what they could do to change what they see as very dangerous turns in the direction of American politics. Although the manuscript has not gone through the standard review process, I have had the very useful advice of friends and former colleagues, most of whom advised me not to be too academic. Well, old habits die hard, but I tried. And I think I have made some of the best analyses of political scientists and professionals accessible if not always exciting. You can skip through some of the material if you like, but if you truly want to work for change I think it will be worth your while to read on. Many of the most sincere and dedicated activists I know are, unfortunately, wasting their time or actually acting in ways that might be counter-productive. Politics remains as much art as science. It is, at the same time, a well-studied activity that operates according to increasingly well-understood rules. While there are no clear rules of political efficacy, there are ways of doing things that are manifestly more effective than others.

I want particularly to thank Ellen Boneparth, Virginia Martin, Gareth Rhodes, Christina Russenello, Elliot Schneier, Jeff Stonecash, Lynda Stratigos and above all my wife Margrit for their help and comments.

Introduction

Putting People Back in Politics

Seldom in American politics has there been an eruption of political activism comparable to that which arose in the wake of the 2016 elections. Literally tens of millions took to the streets and town meetings offering time, money and passion to the causes of peace, good government, civil rights and economic justice. Most of them were wasting their time. In politics, sincerity and conviction win grace points but little influence. Even money– the "mother's milk of politics"– doesn't make much of a difference if it is poorly spent; and the sad fact is that much of it is.

The purpose of this book is to offer a short guide to effective political action, particularly in the realms of political campaigns and legislative advocacy. The premise, that ordinary people can make a difference, has become almost quaint. Political campaigns and political advocacy (also known as lobbying) have been professionalized to the point where citizens are treated more as audiences than participants. This is not to denigrate the skills of political professionals, most of whom are very good at what they do.

In becoming more effective citizens we can learn a lot from those for whom politics is a way to make a living. But in making a case that ordinary people can make a difference, I also want to argue that they should. As smart and capable as most political consultants and lobbyists are, they have become the core actors in an increasingly dysfunctional system. Real change can come only when we put people back in politics.

This short book is written for those who are asking themselves what they can do to help bring the country back– back from the slide toward authoritarianism, back from increasingly bitter and counter-productive partisan posturing, back from anti-intellectual know-nothingism, back from the brink of growing ethnic and racial divisions, and back from growing economic and political inequality.

There are all kinds of ways in which elections are won and lost. Sophisticated uses of polls, social media, computer algorithms and advertising are claimed to be able increasingly to target and deliver blocs of voters to those candidates who can afford them. Campaign management has become a big business. Between elections, similarly sophisticated paid lobbyists exert a strong influence on behalf of those who can best afford to hire them. The premise here, however, is that in the long run nothing works better than a well-organized movement of average citizens. Clever advertising can swing votes, but nothing is more effective than direct contact with someone you already know. Facts and numbers count for a lot in lobbying, as does money; but the stories of informed constituents as to how the law impacts real people in a legislator's district can still carry the day.

In 1970 my then co-author, William T. Murphy, Jr. and

I wrote a book called *Vote Power* as handbook for student volunteers working under the umbrella of the Princeton-based Movement for a New Congress which helped elect a number of anti-war Representatives and Senators in the midterm elections. While the Movement was successful in channeling the energies of activists into electoral politics, it was neither intended nor able to follow up its election victories with policy advocacy. The war dragged on for another four years, and while many of the Senators and House members it helped elect became effective spokespersons for progressive causes, the students who helped elect them, in effect, went back to their classrooms.

Murphy and I published a second edition of the book in 1974 when Nixon's Watergate problems were closing in, and the failure of our intervention in Vietnam was widely perceived. As we moved through the 1970s, however, the allure of citizen participation in politics was fading. A whole new cadre of political campaign professionals took over the management of most state, local and national election campaigns. They replaced the rusty, often moribund party organizations and political machines that had been at core of political campaigns for nearly a century. While few mourned the passing of the Daley organization in Chicago or New York's Tammany Hall, the rise of what became known as "candidate-centered campaigns" took us into a not-so-brave new world of political dysfunction. The premises of *Vote Power,* with its emphasis on face-to-face politics was becoming quaint.

"In the wake of Watergate," Murphy and I wrote in 1974, "political cynicism is reaching an all-time high. No lecture on democratic theory is going to convince many

Americans that corruption is not part and parcel of the electoral process." [1] Forty plus years later, these perceptions have, if anything, become increasingly more negative. Consider the state of our major political institutions. In a 2016 Gallup survey of citizen trust in their political institutions, the Supreme Court and the Presidency were rated "very" or "somewhat" worthy of trust by just 36%; the Congress by just 9%. The last time a majority of Americans trusted the Court was in 2002; the Presidency in 2009; and not once since the 1970s has Congress earned majority support. [2]

Cynicism, doubt and despair, no matter how warranted, are wasted emotions unless backed with incentives to act. And the only kinds of effective acts available to most of us involve working within the institutional structures already in place. We don't need Syria to remind us that armed resistance is fruitless in a garrison state, a "cure" probably worse than the disease. Demonstrations are useful tools of consensus building, publicity and mobilization, but they change nothing. Tea Party demonstrations in 2014 and 2015 did help to create networks of believers, their bonds strengthened by social media that began to bear fruit only when they were linked to political campaigns and backed by the financial and professional resources of very traditional Republican Party and wealthy interest groups. For those seeking change not catharsis, there are really only two kinds of effective political action.

> The two kinds are pressure politics and electoral politics, and I am inclined to think there are no other kinds. To choose

pressure politics means to try to influence those people who already hold power, who sit in official seats, and who may even be responsible for the outrages against which the movement is aimed. To choose electoral politics is to try to dislodge those people and to plant others in their seats. . . . Of course, the two choices overlap in important ways . . . but it is worth emphasizing the two simply because they exhaust the range: changing the policies men [and women] make and changing the men [and women] who make policies. Changing the political system within which policy is made is rarely a real option for citizen activists.[3]

To put a more positive spin on this last point, changing the system in which policy is made *is* possible, but only, ironically, by changing or influencing the people who are already in office. To change the rules of the game, in other words, one must first change the rule-makers. Whatever the social goals which motivate people to involve themselves in politics, the best way to achieve those goals is to elect candidates who share them or to scare the hell out of those who do not. Some politicians are shrewd. Some are simply dumb. Some are corrupt and can be bought. All know how to count votes. Nothing is more important to the future of American society than the way in which those votes are distributed. On election night they don't count issues, preferences or emotions; they count votes. And between elections, politicians don't look back, they think about the next election.

Professionals have important roles to play in campaigns: election laws, particularly those regarding campaign finance are complex and important. Professionals are, by definition, less likely to accept the often-biased assurances of local "leaders" who will say things like "don't worry about the third ward, I've got that covered," or "don't even bother with Mudville, they're all against us." Even in small-town local elections, it is useful to have someone other than the candidate to take the heat for some necessary decisions (like telling the local nutcake why his or her help is not wanted). There is, moreover, a whole library of books, and a large industry of trained and experienced campaign managers who understand how to conduct and use public opinion polls, create effective promotional materials, make media buys, and so on. Even the best managed of these campaigns, however, leave something to be desired, and a strong case can be made the very paradigm on which the professional campaign edifice is built has become increasingly less effective.

The old British adage that trained civil servants should be kept on tap but not on top applies with special force to professional political operatives. For although there are things that require expert knowledge– every campaign, for example, needs access to legal advice, media buys, voter targeting, financial reporting and fund raising– too many modern campaigns are run by very talented people with all these skills but little knowledge of the districts in which they are working. In 2016, there were many active Democrats in Ohio, Pennsylvania and Wisconsin who could have told

Hillary Clinton that her campaign was floundering; her very smart campaign professionals didn't figure that out until election night.

Let us at the outset be very clear about the very real limits of citizen power. Any individual's personal influence is likely to be small. Your vote, in any given election, is unlikely to affect the outcome: in a typical congressional district in 2016 it was as little as 1/350,000th of the total. Many, if not most legislative districts, moreover, have been constructed as to not be competitive. Running against incumbents has always been especially difficult. In 2016, 97% of the members of the House and 93% of Senators running for re-election won. In a polarized polity, moreover, political conversions are rare, the fight is frequently more about who can turn out the faithful. And this is not easy. Non-voters are non-voters for a reason, sometimes out of active hostility to all things political, more frequently out a deep-seated apathy difficult for politically active people to understand.

Equally frustrating for many activists is the discovery that many voters know little about key issues. To those who do, finding someone who agrees with them on most issues but is voting for the opposing candidate because she seems honest, has run a successful business, hasn't had an affair, or who looks like a congressman, can be very frustrating. And then there are the single issue people, found among both voters and volunteers. In most campaigns, you really are selling "lesser-evilism," a pragmatic calculus– all things considered– that voting for one candidate or another will in the long run, considering all issues, make the country a better place. When it works, ours is a representative democracy in which we elect people not to put all of our desires into policy, but to work with others in at least partially satisfying as many as possible. Unless you are looking in a mirror, you will seldom see a perfect candidate, nor will that perfect candidate be able to see all of his or her preferences enacted into law. Vanity voters, who see voting as an expressive rather than instrumental act can be as frustrating as hard core opponents, particularly when they support hopeless third party candidates.

The extreme form of vanity voting is support for third parties. The math is very simple. Let us suppose that you are a Democrat who believes that the "powers that be" in the party keep coming up with candidates who are "too centrist," "too beholden to Wall Street," or whatever, and you are convinced that a third party candidate could win at least a third of the vote. OK, here's the math. Take that third of the total vote (say 33,333 of 100,000) votes in the general election; the "Wall Street Democrat" wins 25,000– pretty good, the two proto-Democrats get better than 58%– but they lose to a Freedom caucus Republican who gets less than 42,000. Instead of a lesser evil Democrat, both the leftists and the centrists wind up being represented by someone they both agree is truly awful. Run that same candidate in the Democratic primary–where far fewer than 50,000 vote– and your 33,000 votes win the nomination in a walk and almost certainly goes on to victory in November.

What most third party advocates and many partisans do not recognize is just how vulnerable the major parties are. While they differ between the parties and among the states, the essential building blocks start at the level of local election districts or precincts where enrolled party members "run" in primaries. Typically, these races are almost never competitive: anyone who can get the ten or twenty signatures to get the nomination will be able to run unopposed. My son and daughter-in-law live in semi-rural district in New Jersey where, typically, six of the eight district committee seats were vacant. My daughter-in law raised her hand and is now vice chair, with four of her progressive allies filling out the slate. Essentially all it takes to become a part of the party "power structure" is to raise your hand. It gets more difficult and complicated as one moves up to the county or ward or assembly district level, then to the state and national committees, but the process at all levels– and in both major parties– is wide open. The real powers of these organizations– especially vis-a-vis incumbent office holders– vary; but they are almost always far more permeable than most outsiders think.

This is not a campaign manual. It doesn't instruct potential candidates how to run, nor does it serve as reference manual for winning campaigns. There are plenty of good books that do that. What it does try to do is to make sense of a political system that is not working very well, and to try to provide some glimmers of hope, and some concrete steps to be taken by those who believe in democratic change. Beyond election-related activities, it is also a roadmap of sorts to political influence between elections. This is not a book for everyone. It is aimed, quite specifically, at those who are frightened, frustrated and flummoxed by Donald Trump's election and that of the members of Congress who have worked with him radically to redirect our politics. It is aimed at those who deplore the development of important public policies– from health care legislation to the legislative budget– behind the closed doors of the majority party caucus with no expert testimony, with no public hearings, and with no inputs from the minority. It is aimed at those who deplore the development of "alternative facts," the rejection of science and "the toxic confluence of arrogance, narcissism and cynicism that Americans now wear like a full suit of armor against experts and professionals."[4] And it is for people who oppose rather than welcome the growing openness and acceptance of racial and ethnic political prejudice. Conservatives may find some of its practical suggestions useful, but will probably find its liberal bias too tendentious to ignore. And that's fine. At this juncture in time, the Democratic Party seems to be the most viable vehicle for implementing change. We can hope that the voices of reason in the Republican Party will re-emerge in the years ahead— some are actually running in 2018— but it is, for now, the ideological rigidity, inflexibility and intolerance of the leadership of the Grand Old Party that makes it more a part of the problem than a likely solution.

Without, I hope, being overly academic I have tried to summarize the best research we have on politically effectiveness. For those with little patience for the soggy details of each topic, I have appended a brief executive summary and action guide to the beginning of each chapter summarizing what individual citizens and voluntary groups can do and what they need to know about putting people back in politics.

Endnotes

1   William T. Murphy, Jr. and Edward Schneier, *Vote Power: How to Work for the Person You Want Elected* (Garden City, NY: Anchor Books, 1974), viii.

2   Http://www.Gallup.com/poll/1597/confidence-institutions.aspx . Accessed, April 25, 2017.

3   Michael Walzer, *Political Action: A Practical Guide to Movement Politics* (Chicago: Quadrangle Books, 1971), 25-26.

4   Tom Nichols, *The Death of Expertise: The Campaign Against Established Knowledge and Why It Matters* (New York: Oxford University Press, 2017), 3.

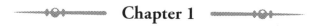

Chapter 1

The Changing Face of American Politics

Executive Summary and Action Plan

Our system of government remains far more open to dedicated activists than most of them believe. The purpose of this chapter is to explain how our system has fallen into an abyss of polarization, dysfunction and mistrust; how our major institutions are failing, and what can be done about it. In section one I make the case that getting involved in politics is important not just in the short run sense of changing public policy, but in the larger sense of putting our democratic system back together. The most viable pathway to change is through electoral politics, and the most accessible vehicle is the Democratic Party.

Section two— the demise of the Democrats— and Section three— on professionalization— explain how the Party, despite a strong edge in public support, has done badly in recent elections. These are somewhat statistical arguments, trying to make sense of an academic literature that provides important counters to some over-simple explanations too often believed. The Democratic Party's slow decline is rooted partially in demographic patterns beyond control; and in part by deliberate gerrymanders and discriminatory election laws, the Electoral College, and a badly skewed system of campaign finance. Many of the Party's problems, however, are of its own making. Its fundamental economic and social justice orientations have been distorted less by substantive policies than through top-down, elitist, money-driven methods of running for office. Although its campaign professionals have developed increasingly sophisticated methods of targeting and delivering voters, the bloodless, impersonal nature of these techniques has robbed the party of authenticity. Only when it puts face-to-face interactions back into the equation can it overcame the electoral disadvantages built into the system.

The first step in putting people back in politics is to revive, replace or displace the many party organizations that have become empty shells. Activists must understand the importance of capturing the nominating process, the most crucial but least understood of aspect of American electoral politics. In most parts of the country, major party nominations can be won, and party organizations taken over with tiny fractions of the popular vote. Effective activism begins here.

In the concluding sections we return to a more academic analysis of how the current system is out of whack. Particularly important for those working in congressional campaigns—potential candidates in particular— many readers may prefer to skip to chapter two.

The 2018 elections provide the opportunity to begin the process of changing the increasingly dysfunctional Congress where the ideal of responsible parties has been distorted into a system of top down leadership that has frozen out, not just Democrats, but the Republican's own rank-and-file as well. Both parties need legislators with ties to their districts strong enough to counter the centralizing forces of party discipline and big money. The failure of Congress to encourage deliberation, specialization, expertise and oversight of the administration has badly distorted the balance of powers in which our constitutional system is grounded. The open deliberation of important issues is both a hallmark of democracy and the road to the restoration of trust in government. The first steps toward reform are those actively involving citizens in politics.

1. The Importance of Participation

One of the few things on which the supporters of the Tea Party, Bernie Sanders, Donald Trump and countless others readily agree is that the American political system is functioning badly. As party polarization has intensified, our sense of a civic culture and its related values of comity, courtesy and compromise have evaporated into a toxic atmosphere of alienation and mistrust. As with most swings in national mood, recent manifestations of dysfunction and discord are most vividly on display in Congress which— to give it its due– has rather faithfully recorded and amplified much of what is wrong with our politics. There is a vicious circle here: "deepening public disillusionment . . . has been both cause and effect of policy paralysis."[1]

The waves of discontent that have roiled American waters have washed over other shores as well, bringing dark undercurrents of authoritarianism and intolerance. After years of touting the spread of democracy, the respected *Journal of Democracy* increasingly features gloomy tales of rising authoritarianism. "Even in some of the richest and most politically stable regions of the world," as one recent essay put it, "it seems as if democracy is in a serious state of disrepair."[2] In both the United States and Europe there is a growing tendency for younger people in particular to describe "having a democratic political system" as a "bad" or "very bad" way to "run the country."[3] An infectious, often prejudiced form of nationalistic xenophobia has re-emerged as a significant political force even in countries long thought to have put that sad story behind them. In most of the world's putative democracies, moreover, recent decades have seen a slow but widespread and continuous decline in citizen participation and trust in political institutions.

There is vicious a circle spinning here: the less people participate in their own governance the less they believe they can. Democratic governance is strongly correlated with participatory cultures: educational systems that encourage dialogue as opposed to rote learning, neighborhood associations that actually meet, businesses in which employers and employees work together, and even social organizations where people learn the skills of working together. From Alexis de Tocqueville's 1835 *Democracy in America* to Robert Putnam's *Bowling Alone,* the link between a vigorous associational life and democracy has long been clear. Civic groups produce "virtuous circles" of trust and habits of accommodation, serving as what Tocqueville called "large free schools" in democracy. Bowling alone, in contrast, as opposed to bowling in a league, provides no such experience.[4] It is through group life and working with others that people become citizens rather than subjects.

Putting people back in politics can have the salutatory effects both of making a democratic system work better and of making people feel better about the way the system works. While those in government– the "establishment" if you will– sometimes lose touch with ordinary people, being on the inside does have the virtue of making manifest the vulnerabilities of the system. I once asked my one-time boss, former Senator Birch Bayh, what made him think he could run for president. "The better I got to know the other people running," he said, "the more I felt that I could do it." The better one knows people in power– whether in business or government– and the better they know their employees and constituents, the more they become "just folks."

Clearly some people have a lot more power and influence than others. And conspiracies, cabals, networks of corruption do exist. But it is more the complexity of power than its concentration that makes a system dysfunctional and difficult to change. The greater the power distance between citizens and their government, the less likely either is to work well. The first step on the road to closing this gap is to understand the system's complexity and the points of access the system presents. The most accessible pathway to change in 2018 is through electoral politics and the vehicle of the Democratic Party. Only if and when Democrats are back on track is there any hope of reforming the Republican Party and of putting ordinary people back in politics.

2. The Demise of the Democrats

Democrats have had at least a slight advantage in the percentage of people identifying with a party almost every year since Gallup began surveying party preferences in 1991. As of 2017, however, Republicans controlled the White House, the House of Representatives, the Senate, 32 of 50 Governorships and 67 of 98 partisan state legislative houses. Their margin of seats in state legislatures is now 4100 to 3200, despite the edge Democrats still enjoy in party registrations. Clearly the Democrats are being outplayed.

In part, the Democrats misfortunes are rooted in demographics. Urban areas and areas of high poverty remain at the core of the party's voting constituency. These voters are concentrated to the extent that they form what amounts to a natural gerrymander in what academics call partisan clustering. Gerrymandering works by maximizing seats in the legislature by winning a lot of districts by small margins and losing a few by landslides. By concentrating all or most of the voters of one party in the same district, many of their votes are in effect "wasted." In the 2016 elections for the State Senate in New York, to use a fairly typical example, 22 of the 31 Democrats elected (20 of them in New York City) won with 90% of the vote or more. Only 6 of 30 Republicans won by similarly lopsided margins, or, to put it another way, it took the Republicans fewer votes to win more seats. Although there is a gerrymandering factor that explains the Republican's ability to maintain control of the

State Senate, partisan clustering is also a strong influence.[5] Democratic voters are clustered in urban areas less by gerrymandering than by patterns of residency founded in economics, ethnicity, race and choice. Nationally, a similar combination of gerrymandering and demographics has produced a House of Representatives in which "very few representatives (twenty-nine to be precise) now serve in districts without a clear partisan tilt."[6]

Economic segregation has also impacted the Democratic vote by creating a "class gap" in participation. Poorer neighborhoods, with fewer competitive elections and less vibrant civic cultures, lack the political resources and skills more readily available to the affluent. This gap "helps perpetuate a virtuous cycle of engagement and responsiveness among the prosperous and a vicious cycle of isolation and disengagement among the impoverished."[7] And this has helped create a parallel problem for the Party. "The economic segregation of wealth has made it easier and less costly to target neighborhoods with stronger civic environments– specifically, robust social networks, active voluntary associations and higher levels of education and income."[8] Add to this increasingly expensive campaigns that rely on affluent donors, and the Democrats, as a party, find themselves increasingly distanced from their base. Republicans, meanwhile, have been increasingly aggressive in using their new majorities, particularly at the state level, to aggravate this gap by revising the rules of the game in their favor. Adding deliberate gerrymanders to demographic disparities they have virtually locked in their legislative majorities. Further tipping the balance, they have enacted state-level election rules specifically aimed at disenfranchising the poor, particularly those in urban areas.[9]

The cumulative effects of these factors are striking. In most elections since the Supreme Court ruled that districts must be of roughly equal size, the party winning the most popular votes usually won a bonus of a few seats in the House. In 1996, however, the Democrats won a majority of the total popular vote, but only 47.6% of House seats. Only once since then (in 2008) have Democrats won a higher percentage of seats than votes, and the differential is growing. In 2014, Republicans won 56.8% of the seats with only 53% of the vote. In 2016, the Democrats total of 48.9% of the major party congressional vote gained them only 44.6% of the seats– the biggest discrepancy between seats and votes (4.3%) in modern history.[10]

As much as these factors help explain the Democrats under-performance in recent elections, many of the larger problems are of their own making. Since the election of Donald Trump, Democrats have been arguing about the message the party should be sending to voters. To critics of the Party's "establishment," its leadership has been too close to Wall Street and too far from tapping into the aspirations of its economically deprived base voters. If the Democrats moved to the left, it is argued, if they more vigorously espoused policies that redistribute income, they could have won major victories in 2016. "If only" questions are always problematic in politics; but his one, despite its apparent simplicity, is particularly opaque.

To begin with, voters had no problem distinguishing Clinton and Trump on economic issues, and they did so by margins that make it difficult to argue that a change in either candidates' positions on economic issues could substantially have changed the outcome.[11] Among voters with incomes of less than $50,000, Clinton trailed Obama's 2012 percentage by 7 percent, but still beat Trump 53% to 41%. Some proportion of this fall-off is explained by the lower turnouts of African Americans, but the dominant narrative of the campaign– that the Democrats lost because they failed to reach working class and lower income voters– is, at best, weakly supported. Gallup researchers found, for example, that although Trump did slightly better in areas of "diminished economic activity," his supporters were in those areas were more likely themselves to be employed, and to have a median income $15,000 above the national median.

It may well be that Bernie Sanders, absent the burdens of Benghazi, etc. could have run a stronger campaign than Hillary Clinton. But the effects of the Senator's liabilities, the skeletons in his political closet that were not raised in the primaries, are unknown, and the fact that he could win less than 43% of the total vote among Democrats in the primaries, suggest that he would have, at best, done no better than Clinton in the general. Polls taken during the campaign rather consistently showed issues of "character" and recondite but apparently significant "issues" such as Benghazi and Clinton's e-mails often exceeding economic concerns in the eyes of voters, particularly among those with lower incomes and education. And when Clinton moved left to adopt positions similar to those of Bernie Sanders on college tuition, the effects on public opinion were negligible. Congressional candidates who ran to the left of Clinton, moreover, did not run particularly well. Clinton lost Wisconsin, for example, by a margin of just 23,000 votes; but the progressive Russ Feingold lost his Senate race by 99,000. Ted Strickland, similarly lost his Ohio race by 11.4% compared with Clinton's 8.6.

If economic issues had few direct effects in 2016, perceptions did. And it could well be that it was less Clinton's actual stands than perceptions of her "real" loyalties and positions that hurt most. Robert Reich put it as follows:

> The Democratic Party as it is now constituted has become a giant fundraising machine, too often reflecting the goals and values of the moneyed interests. This must change. . . .The election of 2016 has repudiated it. We need a people's party — a party capable of organizing and mobilizing Americans in opposition to Donald Trump's Republican Party... What happened in America Tuesday should not be seen as a victory for hatefulness over decency. It is more accurately understood as a repudiation of the American power structure.[12]

This brings us a lot closer to understanding why Clinton, and Democrats more generally, did so badly in 2016 and how the situation can be improved. The Democrat's message can be tinkered with for sure, a task made both easier and more urgent as Tea Party/Trump policies unfold. Unfortunately, however, the Party's fundamental economic and social justice orientation has been distorted less by substantive policies than through its top-down, elitist, money-driven methods of running for office. The medium, to recycle Marshall McLuhan's aphorism, has become the message. The modern campaign, whether at the national, state or local level; whether Republican or Democratic, has become more a technology-intensive bureaucratic battle of campaign professionals than a contest between politicians, partisans and political activists.

3. The Professionalization of Politics

In the 1950s and 60s, spurred by the emergence of television as a cultural influence, a new kind of politics emerged in the United States. Party organizations were increasingly replaced by candidate-centered coalitions run by an increasingly specialized cadre of campaign professionals. The whole hierarchy of party leaders, from precinct captains to ward leaders to state chairs was displaced by "nearly 75 different categories of campaign professionals, including crisis management, grassroots strategy, digital mapping, media and speech training, online information services, referendum consulting, and more."[13] The modern campaign begins with fund-raising which often precedes the selection of staff. One professional campaign consultant told me recently that he wouldn't work for a congressional candidate who hadn't already raised at least $200,000. The next step, as a rule, is to hire professionals and commission a poll. Candidate polls– unlike the horse race-who's ahead polls you find in the media– are directed less at questions of who is winning than on how various demographic groups are likely to respond to particular kinds of appeals. From a mass media approach, where the goal was to maximize exposure of the campaign message, "a carefully honed message is directed to each persuadable voter group. Contemporary electioneering uses a rifle, not a shotgun. It is the art and science of modern campaign 'targeting.'"[14] Gone is good-old-Charlie who knew everyone in the Fifth Ward. Instead there are experts in data analytics, many of whom have no real knowledge of, or particular interest in politics and public policy. Candidates too have changed. Once there was a more or less regular progression up the political ladder from party work to local and state offices and on to Congress or the state legislature. In recent sessions of Congress, for the first time in modern history, fewer than half of the members of the House and Senate had served previously in state legislatures.[15] More lateral entry, by-passing party organizations in favor of candidates with money and celebrity appeal has shifted the ground from debates and press reports to campaign controlled paid media. In the extreme case, candidates seldom appear anywhere but at their own tightly scripted events.

Modern campaign technologies are often criticized for packaging candidates as if they were toothpaste or soap. In fact what professional campaigns package are voters. Polls are the first step. These can provide nice numbers to bring to potential campaign donors, but the usual campaign poll is less about who will when than how. What the campaign survey seeks to find are key blocs of voters and the issues and channels of communication that can best reach them. If, for example, one finds that suburban women have a distinctive preference for a particular policy, you locate media– whether on the internet, through direct mail, radio or whatever– that have a distinctively suburban female audience. If your candidate is way ahead among Polish Americans, you direct get-out-the-vote efforts to voters with Polish names.

Polling, however, has significant (and growing) limitations. In just over a decade, the percentage of households using cell phones as opposed to land lines has gone from near zero to nearly sixty percent. Since federal law prohibits robo-dialing to cell phones, reaching voters has become considerably more expensive, though still doable. What are much harder to overcome are the biases that come from systems that identify or block calls, and from the growing number of people who refuse to be surveyed. Adjustments can be made. One source of error in the 2016 surveys in some states, for example, was the failure of some pollsters to take into consideration different response rates associated with education.[16] It is possible to correct such errors by (the expensive way) polling more people or by statistically "adjusting" the results by giving added weight to less educated respondents; but the more you do this, the less "random" your sample and the less reliable the results.

It gets worse. In the campaign poll, as opposed to one simply measuring who's ahead, it is the subcategories that are of prime concern. With gender dividing half male and half female, a sample of 1200 now becomes 600 which still yields an acceptable margin of error; but if you want to check, say urban, suburban and rural women, or low, high and medium income males, the cell sizes shrink to the point where the margins of error can go up to double digits. And if you to pull out, say Latino, middle income males you may be making inferences from the responses of as few as a dozen people, not a reliable sample at all.

Good pollsters have developed increasingly sophisticated

methods for dealing with these problems and others; but the inherent limitations of the process have fostered the development of complex data banks and algorithms that combine poll data, canvassing results, computer site selections, demographics and campaign donation records, and even such things as membership in the Audubon Society to identify communities of identity, interest, emotion, affinity and peer networks that can be used to identify, target, package and deliver voters.[17] These high technology techniques have revolutionized electoral politics to the point at which the "post-modern" candidate is more a piece "in a complex communication environment, rather than driving these developments."[18] Extend this argument only slightly, and it suggests that we have moved to a system in which it is the campaigns rather than the candidates that are the driving forces.

The post-modern campaign both replicates and improves upon the ward politics of old by, in effect, changing the concept of the ward from that of a geographic unit to a social network constituted through technology. "While the 'wards' of the past were defined geographically and at times as legal units of political representation, today they are expansive spaces of mediated social relations that encompass the geographic communities, families, professional and identity affiliations, and acquaintances of supporters."[19] The interactions between and among these networks, at the same time, are not the kinds of unmediated communications that take place face to face. They are essentially bloodless, more in the nature of semi-connected monologues than human conversations. Thus although there is little doubt that technology can dramatically expand the scope of political communications and the size of the community, it is not at all clear that there is any real dialogue taking place. Theda Skocpol, Harvard Professor of Government and Sociology, puts this in personal terms:

> Every month or so, I get a letter from some Democratic Party office: a long, canned statement, hopelessly bland, accompanied by a fake questionnaire, a tear-out wallet "membership card," and– of course, the real point– a return card and envelope for me to use to send a big check. The party tells me, in the form letter, that it wants my opinions. But it really just wants my money so it can pay pollsters and consultants. In turn, party officials, or consultants hired by the party, tell individual candidates how to word their media messages and speeches. . . The consultants pretty much are the Democratic Party. In most communities and states, there are few opportunities for regular Democrats to talk with one another, or to talk back to the consultants and candidates. The people who talk to one another are the consultants.[20]

It need not work this way. The new technologies can be used in ways that supplement and strengthen rather than displace volunteers on the ground. With help from the data bases, volunteers can have "more information at their fingertips than they would have with conventional walk lists, including basic information on members of their neighbors' households (e.g., ages, party affiliation, registration status, and the results of prior canvasses)."[21] At the same time, continuing tensions between number crunchers and amateurs and between national organizations and local forces are inevitable, as are, what one of Obama's key advisors described as a tension between "the desire to be authentic and the desire to be super-duper effective."[22]

4. Learning from Tammany Hall

The old machines died for a number of reasons. A better educated electorate increasingly rejected their paternalistic culture. The welfare state made their direct help to the needy less necessary. As incomes rose, their patronage jobs became less attractive. And their own excesses increasingly made them targets of ridicule and scorn. In a larger sense, however, the interpersonal, face-to-face politics of the old organizations lost its relevance to a more mobile, media-oriented politics. Despite these shifts, the formal organizational structures of the major parties remain essentially unchanged. The basic building block of the organization was and still is the precinct (sometimes known as an election district), usually composed of roughly a thousand registered voters, whose party members elect two captains. These precinct captains typically meet at least once a year to elect the next level of officers, which are called county committee members in some areas, ward leaders in many urban areas, or district leaders (covering, for example, the districts used to elect members of the state assembly). They in turn elect the members of the state committees of each party, who in turn elect representatives to the national committees. In their day, strong party organizations like New York's Tammany Hall, the Daley organization in Chicago, the Republican organizations on New York's Long Island, and the Cox machine in Cincinnati, Ohio decided who would run as the party's candidates; who would get jobs in city, county and, sometimes, state offices; and, frequently, who would win government contracts. Often corrupt, these party machines nonetheless played an important role, particularly in the early 1900s in bringing immigrants into the system; bringing order to fragmented, ineffective governments; and "providing avenues of social mobility for the otherwise disadvantaged."[23] There are virtually no effective political machines, Republican or Democratic, in the United States today; but there are still lessons to be learned from both their successes and failures and in comparison with the campaign systems that displaced them.

The problem of the typical machine politician was his or her inability to move past organizational norms more oriented toward favor trading and patronage than good public policy. The machine, however, knew that its survival depended on its ability to nominate candidates who were both loyal and (more importantly) electable. The problem with today's self-recruited candidate is that he or she might not be either.

The beginning point of wisdom for citizen activists is the importance of recapturing the nominating process.

Many years ago, one of the sharpest of the old machine's practitioners, Frank Kent, pointed out that if the organization "loses in the primaries, it is out of business."[24] So it remains today with anyone seeking political power.

In all but a handful of states, "candidates of the two great parties must first be nominated as a result of primaries."[25] It is a continuing source of wonder how few Americans understand this basic fact. By refusing to register with a party, almost a third of all voters have given up their right to participate in this process.[26] Of those allowed to vote in primaries, moreover, it is striking how few do. Here is a case from my co-authored text on New York politics that is extreme but illustrative. It involves Patrick Manning, a member of the New York State Assembly, who for years had run unopposed in either the primary or general election.

> When Manning embarked on a brief campaign for governor in 2006, a local mayor decided to challenge him in the Republican primary for his assembly seat. Fewer than 6,000 voters turned out in the September primary, giving the upstart, Marcus Molinaro of Tivoli, the Republican line by a margin of just 2,770 to 2,539. Molinaro's opponent in the November general election was an unusually vigorous and articulate candidate, but despite lingering divisions in the Republican Party, she lost to Molinaro by a margin of 22,065 to 17,531.[27]

Look carefully at these numbers. The 103rd Assembly District had a total of 70,387 registered Republicans. To win the primary, in other words, Molinaro needed to win the support of just four percent of the district's Republican voters. To put it another way, he needed just twenty-six votes in each of the two counties' 104 election districts to win. In the days of the old machine, that was pretty easy: each of the two precinct captains was expected to cast his or her vote for the machine candidate and bring in at least three or four relatives each– ten votes without leaving the house, just sixteen more needed to win. Add in a few holders of patronage jobs and their relatives, or maybe friends from the local tavern or coffee shop, and the job was done. If those fairly automatic votes for the old machine are harder to come by in the twenty-first century, the basic math is a constant: find an organizer in each election district who can round up twenty-five or more voters and you're in the game. Now New Yorkers might not be good at voting in primaries (the elections that count) as opposed to wasting their votes in November when it usually does not. In Colorado in 2016, for example, Darryl Green needed 43 votes per precinct in the Republican primary contest to take on the Democratic incumbent Michael Bennet (he lost in November). But Tammy Duckworth won her Democratic primary for the Senate in Illinois with just 26 votes per election district and went on to win in the general election. There are districts like these throughout the country, for Congress sometimes, for state offices almost always. As much as the parties may "largely nullify each other's effectiveness," in November, in the primaries "the machines have no organized competition. Hence they become enormously effective and, so long as the average voter fails to participate, are practically invincible."[28] The point here, which we will elaborate on in Chapter three, is that the decline of the regular party organizations has left a void that can be filled.

The final, and still enduring point that Kent made with regard to primaries, is that "members of the state central committee, control of which is key to the whole machine, are elected in the primaries."[29] Those who charged during or after the 2016 elections that the system is somehow rigged have only their own passivity or ignorance of the process to blame. It is either ignorance of the law or innumeracy that would lead one to register as an independent, or organize a third party campaign for the general election when the major parties are so open to challenge in their primaries.

Even at the national level, looking back to 2016, although there is no hard evidence of DNC interference in the presidential primaries or caucuses, there is no doubt that there was a Clinton bias at the higher levels of the DNC; but whatever the biases various state committees and the national committees may have had, they were there because Democrats– or, more correctly, Democrats who voted in party primaries– put them there. For most of its history the Republican and Democratic National Committees were noteworthy less for their powers than an almost total lack of real influence. The truth is that at the national level (and indeed in most states) the Democratic Party had little presence as an organized entity, and very little influence with Democratic voters. In some states, the state committees held statewide conventions to endorse candidates, but these endorsements were only sporadically effective. Contrary to its name, moreover, the DNC has almost never acted as the national headquarters of the party (nor has its Republican counterpart played such a role).

Historically, then, the DNC was one player a fragmented party. Its chief and almost exclusive function was that of raising the money, largely from interest groups, to underwrite the national convention every four years and support its presidential nominee. The efforts of both the Republican and Democratic National Committees to play more active roles were largely thwarted both at the national level by each party's Senate and House campaign committees, and at the state and local level by party organizations that see such activity as interference rather than help. As one textbook put it, "Where the party organizations of many other Western democracies have had permanent, highly professional leadership and large party bureaucracies, most American party organizations, especially at the local level, are still in the hands of part-time activists.[30]

There is no doubt that his is changing. After his unsuccessful 2004 run for President, former Vermont Governor Harold Dean brought some of his most savvy political technicians to the DNC. As its new Chairman, Dean "worked out a deal in which the national party assumed the costs of improving and maintaining the state voter files and building a new data base to house them, in exchange for permission to aggregate and extend them."[31] Through Dean's "Vote Builder" program, endorsed Democratic candidates have access to continuously updated files of quality data on states or districts. While the Republicans were a little slower to adopt these technologies, the two parties are now pretty much on par. Who controls these valuable lists and how they will be used, as we shall see in chapters two and three, remain open questions that the state and national parties along with individual candidates have yet to effectively answer.

Perhaps the most significant and also unresolved change

in the role of the party's national committees derive from a two decisions of the Supreme Court. The infamous *Citizens United* and a too-little noticed 2014 decision *McCutcheon v. FEC*. *Citizens United* allowed individuals to give unlimited, anonymous contributions to Political Action Committees not working with specific campaigns. In *McCutcheon* the Court ruled that Congress could not limit the aggregate amount of donations from any given individual to more than one campaign or party organization. Thus limits on how much one could contribute to a single campaign or party group are legal, but overall limits are not. So what many multi-millionaires now do is to donate the maximum allowable amount each to a number of state party organizations that then transfer the money to the national committees which can then send them to individual candidates and thus effectively avoid donation limits. Through these devices it has been estimated that more than a third of all money raised in 2016 came from as few as fifty mega-donors. What has been less frequently observed is the markedly enhanced role this gives the national party organizations in directing the flow of campaign giving by the super-rich.

The unresolved question both with regards to voter lists and money is whether and how the national committees will use these new sources of leverage more actively to recruit candidates and micro-manage local campaigns. Not surprisingly, many state and local party organizations believe, rightly in my opinion, that the national committees are insufficiently acquainted with local politics to make these decisions. This brings us back to the importance of putting people back in politics, either by taking over largely ineffectual formal party organizations or by setting up parallel structures to make strong and affirmative pre-primary endorsements.

5. The F(l)ailing Federal Government

Article I one of the Constitution makes the Congress the primary engine of national politics. It has become the caboose. It is lot easier, as the late Speaker of the House "Tip" O'Neill put it, to burn down a barn than to build one. Conservative Republicans, long in the barn burning tradition of the party out of power, proved the utility of O'Neill's adage in their fight against the Affordable Health Care Act. Far more fun it was, with a veto-armed Obama in the White House, to whoop through a monthly vote of legislative arson than to build a workable alternative when they took control of all three branches. Their problems in constructing new programs, however, were not rooted entirely in either the complexity of the issues nor the Republican's lack of experience in policy-marking. They were instead the product of a long-term secular decline in the capacity of the Congress to fulfill its proper role in our political system. Not only is Congress "The Broken Branch," as Thomas Mann and Norman Ornstein's 2006 book called it, but– as in the title of their 2012 follow up– "It's Even Worse than It Looks."[32]

Perhaps the most disingenuous of all the postmortems on the ill-fated "American Health Care Act" was the White House's lame attempt to blame its defeat on the Democrats whose House and Senate members were totally isolated from the bill drafting process, never consulted, never lobbied by the White House. The 2009 process that produced the original bill was partisan. But if the 2009 process was baroque, it was a model of rectitude compared with 2017. Unlike 2009, when three House and two Senate committees each held two months of hearings, there were no hearings– meaning no administration experts, no health care professionals, no lobbyists, no economists– openly consulted eight years later. Unlike 2009, when more than 500 amendments were considered in two Senate committees, and when a Republican alternative bill was debated on the House floor, there were no bipartisan considerations of the bill in either House in 2017.

We have clearly come a long way since 1885 when Woodrow Wilson's classic study of congressional government complained about the "imperious authority of the standing committees."[33] Wilson, in fact, did not have it entirely right: even as he wrote the House Speakers of the nineteenth century were expanding their powers. They continued to do so until 1910 when the revolt against Speaker Cannon led to a reassertion of committee power. Franklin Roosevelt's domination of the system, particularly during the years of World War II, and the expanded role of government that his New Deal had put in place, led the Congress seriously to reexamine its role and structure. The bi-partisan Legislative Reorganization Act of 1946 streamlined the committee system, added professional staff assistants for both committees and individual members, and created a much expanded subcommittee system. To the frustration of President Truman, the newly assertive Congress, its committees dominated by high seniority, conservative southern Democrats, became more of an obstacle than ally to the President's domestic agenda.

My friend and one-time co-author, the late Bertram Gross, was then the chief of staff in Harry Truman's Council of Economic Advisors. Prodded by Truman's frequent complaints about the "phony" Democrats from the south, Gross, Paul David, E. E. Schattschneider and a bi-partisan group of distinguished political scientist created the American Political Science Association's Committee on Political Parties. Its 1950 report, "Toward a More Responsible Two-Party System" argued that, "An effective party system requires, first, that the parties are able to bring forth programs to which they commit themselves and, second, that the parties possess sufficient internal cohesion to carry out these programs."[34] Although Truman's desire to flush out the Southern Democrats was only accomplished inadvertently when the civil and voting rights laws of 1964-65 encouraged conservative, southern whites to become Republicans, the Congress had changed. A landslide Democratic victory in 1964 brought a large class of reform-minded freshmen to Capitol Hill that began dislodging the southern oligarchy and replacing the seniority system with open elections for committee and subcommittee chairs.[35] In 1970, liberals in the Democratic caucus pushed through a package of further reforms, most of them aimed at opening the legislative process to public scrutiny. The democratization of the House spread to the Senate in more limited form, curtailing the ability of small groups to block action through filibusters and other dilatory devices. In both houses, the net effect of the reforms was to spread the action from the old seniority leaders to the rank and file and, in particular, to policy entrepreneurs at the subcommittee level. In political science articles and books it became known as the era of "subcommittee government."

This dispersal of legislative power maximized Congress's ability to mobilize expert knowledge. At its best, subcommittee government encouraged members to become specialists in particular aspects of public policy and gave them the staff resources effectively to oversee the bureaucracy and respond knowledgeably to special interest pressures. Less positively, it helped reinforce what have been called "sub-governments," "whirlpools of influence," or "cozy little triangles," invisible triangles of interacting interest groups, specialized bureaucracies, and their related subcommittees that fragmented both politics and public policy. The longer the members of these policy triangles worked together, the more the subcommittees developed "sympathy-interest-leniency syndromes"[36] that sometimes ignored the public interest.

Subcommittee government tended to tilt toward liberal government, or at least the kind of liberalism that Lowi labeled "interest group liberalism" in which "actual policy-making will not come from voter preference or congressional enactment but from a process of tripartite bargaining between the specialized administrators, relevant members of Congress, and the representatives of self-selected organized interests."[37] As the political center began to shift to the right, this kind of politics became less popular; and even among liberals it became increasingly apparent that this fragmented form of policy-making distorted national priorities. This gave the old notion of responsible party government new legs. Particularly under the leadership of

Speaker Jim Wright the majority House Democrats began significantly to expand the powers of the party leadership.

In 1994, Republican Newt Gingrich brilliantly expanded on Wrights' initiatives to offer a coherent legislative agenda– much like the responsible parties ideal– by offering a "contract for America" and, following an election in which his party won control of the House, reforms to implement it. Gingrich's years as Speaker (1995-99) essentially can be seen as the fulcrum point in the changing balance point between party and subcommittee government. The subsequent strengthening of party leadership transformed the House and strongly influenced the Senate.

> Political parties in Congress no longer act mainly as facilitators of legislative debate and executors of legislative procedures. Now more than ever, the congressional parties act in multiple and independent partisan capacities– setting the partisan agenda, building partisan floor coalitions, getting out the partisan message, undermining the opposition party's reputation, and funding the permanent and costly campaign for majority party control.[38]

Though former Speaker Dennis Hastert personally denies ever having created it, the Republicans have enforced the so-called Hastert rule with a vengeance. Under this formula, no bill is allowed to the floor of the House without sufficient votes in the Republican caucus to pass it without help. The real work of the House, in other words, was shifted from committee rooms and the house floor to the closed meetings of party leaders. On major issues, the Republicans not only froze House Democrats out of any significant role, but most of their own rank-and-file members as well.

With most backbench members having no role whatsoever in major legislation, they spend less time in Washington, have fewer committee meetings and meet largely for show. Particularly among the newer Republican members, some lobbyists say, there are no member staff persons able to talk about substantive policies. In my brief tenure as Birch Bayh's legislative assistant in 1963-64, I handled most of his work on the Public Works Committee and its subcommittee working on the nation's first comprehensive air and water pollution control. After a series of public hearings on an early draft of the bill, the subcommittee held more than forty mark-up sessions of one to three hours each literally rewriting the bill line by line. There was bias in the experts consulted: few environmental groups were organized in those days, and such old-line industries as petroleum, coal, steel and chemicals were probably over-influential. There is little doubt, however, that the law eventually enacted– if it could be criticized for not going far enough– was technically, administratively and legally sound, a claim that few more recent laws can claim

Committee work such as this is important first, for involving both parties and diverse points of view; for invoking "technical expertise, precision in language, and significant policy research; and, finally, for producing "informed and informative" policy.[39] Subcommittee members develop both increasing interest in and aptitude for effective oversight of administration; but as William

Bendix shows, the kinds of markup sessions that produced these results are now rare. "House and Senate committees are omitted from bill development when their ideological composition undermines their ability to operate as reliable instruments of the majority party."[40]

Individual members, in this system, have few incentives or opportunities to develop policy skills. The goals of legislators, it is generally agreed, are re-election, influence within the House, and making good public policy (however defined). Despite increasing polarization, however, and a more ideological politics, the goal of making good public policy has become increasingly nugatory. Decent Republicans and conservative Democrats are on notice that their chances for advancement in the legislative hierarchy are dependent on party loyalty and their ability to raise money, and that while they may be able to cast an independent vote if it necessary for re-election, when the chips are down they must go along to get along. The leadership is increasingly able to provide or withhold campaign funds and other electoral resources. And by rolling bills that used to be in the jurisdictions of four or five committees into omnibus bills, all drafted by central staff, they make it all but impossible for individual members to represent their home districts and states. "Omnibus legislating moves lawmaking behind closed doors. Rank-and-file members are given few if any opportunities to change the final package. More errors, mistakes, and waste may creep into the final legislation as a result."[41]

Congressmen frequently rail against bureaucracy, yet it is in large part their inattention to legislative detail that makes the administrative process important. Simply put, the more detailed the legislation, the less the need for administrative regulations to fill in the blanks. As legislation is drafted with increasingly less care, and as Congress as a whole is too dysfunctional to pass any legislation dealing with such emerging problems as cyberwar, the executive branch has filled the void. Questions of who gets what benefits and how, of how contracts are awarded, of which infrastructure projects will go forward– once the guarded perquisites of legislative committees— are increasingly decided by party leaders or left to administrative discretion. The decline of subcommittees, moreover, has seriously weakened the effectiveness of administrative oversight, the intermittent use of hearings an investigations to control the bureaucracy

6. Responsible Parties?

The two major parties are in many ways more powerful and more sharply differentiated than ever before. From tax policies to spending plans, environmental issues and civil rights to net neutrality, the differences between the parties have been vividly displayed. Republican candidates for Congress– particularly those in marginal districts– often attempt to blur these sharp differences, but once in Congress they vote with the leadership every time it counts. Only when party leaders have all the votes they need to win are the moderates allowed to vote their consciences or their districts. They will, in the pithy words of Barney Frank "give you ice water in January."

Isn't this what the reformers of the 1950s were calling for? Not really. Much of today's polarization is founded less in programmatic differences than in more formidable affective feelings of enmity. "Partisans today are polarized not in their policy preferences but rather in their feelings about each other."[42] Poll data continue to show that most Americans share relatively moderate views on most major issues, and at the same time significant "evidence of polarization in partisans' feelings about the other party. This has caused trust in government to polarize because people do not tend to trust things that are run by people they don't like."[43] Real differences between the parties, moreover,

> Are often obscured by a politics of spin that emphasizes harsh and bitter personal attacks fueled by large sums of cold hard cash. Money and special interests seem more important than at any time since the early twentieth century. The frail public support for parties, the dominance of candidate-centered politics, the Supreme Court's endorsement of a radically individualized politics, and a news media committed to attacking the parties hardly make for a strong party system that might induce a new sense of responsibility into politics and government.[44]

The idea of responsible parties was that strong party organizations, built from the ground up, would– like the old machines but without the glue of patronage– build more or less cohesive coalitions that could hold their elected representatives responsible.

Today's party lines, in contrast, are driven from the

top down, lubricated by an increasingly centralized system of campaign finance that pipes the tunes of programmatic agendas. With responsible parties, party cohesion is more a function of shared goals than fear of discipline.[45] In the contemporary Congress, it is more the fear of sanctions and withheld rewards that explains party unity. The Supreme Court's dismantling of campaign finance laws has accelerated the potential for central control: big donors can far more efficiently "invest" in a single source than sift through hundreds of supplicants for their campaign support. In 2017, Maine Senator Susan Collins courageously defied her party leaders to vote against her party's repeal of the Affordable Care Act. When many provisions of the repeal bill were then folded into the Republican tax reform bill, Collins indicated her intention to vote against that bill unless they were removed. They were not, yet Collins voted aye. The best guess is that Collins was warned she would have a well-funded primary opponent if she didn't toe the line. Is this the future of our politics?

There are limits on the national parties' ability to control the electoral process. Each party has, in reality, three central committees and fifty potential state rivals; each with their own political concerns. Despite the obvious tilt of the Democratic National Committee toward Clinton, it had to remain relatively prudent in practice as the primaries and caucuses unfolded. And the more active attempt by the Republican National Committee to stop Trump shows why. But the nationalization of our party system– generated in no small part by the flow of big money– continues apace in ways that the advocates of responsible parties never imagined. Particularly when the professed objective of the party controlling one or both houses of Congress is to frustrate the president– as it was in the Obama years– the resulting legislative deadlock leaves much of the responsibility for responding to new policy challenges in the hands of the bureaucracy.

Because of such well-publicized acts as Obama's Deferred Action for Childhood Arrivals and Trump's subsequent repeal of it, it appears as if Executive Orders have become more common. Far more common, actually, are rulings by other top executives, cabinet officers, in particular that redefine and elaborate the vagaries of statute law, and memorandums from the White House to various agencies such as Trump's January 2017 imposition of a hiring freeze in all agencies save the Department of Defense. The administration can also put its own spin on existing laws, as the Obama administration did in using bank regulation law as a vehicle for curbing pay day lenders, and the Trump administration did in repealing them. And by simply refusing to fill vacancies in their offices, Secretary of State Tillerson effectively abolished American representation on United States participation in United Nation's bodies dealing with democratization, human rights, the environment and human trafficking.

"It is difficult," Phillip Cooper puts it, "to criticize the president for using various power tools against Congress instead of participating in good faith in the evolution of legislation if the Congress is prepared to suspend its own rules to write legislation on the floor without recourse to normal subcommittee and committee processes."[46] There are serious consequences for the system that flow from the suspension and evasion of democratic procedures. The open deliberation of important public policy issues is not just a hallmark of democracy, but the road to the restoration of trust in government. The first steps toward the restoration of our system are those of once again actively involving citizens in politics, not just in getting people elected, but in staying involved with those they have put in office.

The philosopher Emmanuel Kant's categorical imperative suggests that the moral foundation of a good society begins with treating other people as ends not means. Even more fundamentally, it involves relating to others as real people and not abstractions. To the extent that the modern political campaign packages voters it is morally deficient. To the extent that it manipulates symbols of enmity and division it dehumanizes our politics. Putting people back in politics is a moral imperative. It is also smart politics.

Endnotes

1   Gary W. Reichard, *Deadlock and Disillusionment: American Politics since 1968* (Malden, MA: John Wiley and Sons, 2016), 334.

2   Robert Stefan Foa and Yascha Mounk, "The Democratic Discontent," 27 *Journal of Democracy* (July 2016), 6.

3   Ibid. 9.

4   Alexis de Tocqueville's *Democracy in America* is available in a number of formats. Robert D. Putnam, *Bowling Alone: The Collapse and Revival of American Community* (New York: Simon and Schuster, 2000).

5   The New York case has many parallels, particularly in states with large urban areas. For tests of the impact of partisan gerrymanders and a relatively simple method for determining them, see Samuel H.-S. Wang, "Three Tests for Practical Evaluation of Partisan Gerrymandering," 68 *Stanford Law Review* (June 2016), 1263-91.

6   Gary C. Jacobson and Jamie L. Carson, *The Politics of Congressional Elections* (Lanham, MD: Rowman and Littlefield, 2016), 23.

7   Amy Widestrom, *Displacing Democracy: Economic Segregation in America* (Philadelphia: University of Pennsylvania Press, 2015), 5.

8   Ibid. 183.

9   Zoltan Hajnal, Nazita Najevardi and Lindsay Nielson, "Voter Identification Laws and the Suppression of Minority Votes," 79 *Journal of Politics* (April 2017), 363-79.

10 Special Memo, *Gerrymandering Increasingly Defies the Will of Voters* (Washington: National Committee for an Effective Congress, May, 2017).

11 These figures, and some of those which follow, are derived from exit polls as reported in Larry J. Sabato, "The 2016 Election That Broke All, or At Least Most of the Rules," Larry J. Sabato, Kyle Kondik and Geoffrey Skelley, *Trumped: the 2016 Election That*

Broke All of the Rules (Lanham, MD: Rowman and Littlefield, 2017), pp. 24-27.

12 Quoted in Conor Lynch, "Neoliberalism's Epic Fall," accessed May9, 2017 at http://www.salon.com/2016/11/19/ neoliberalisms-epic-fail-the-reaction-to-hillary-clintons-loss-exposed-the-impotent-elitism-of-liberalism

13 Donald M. Shea and Michael John Burton, *Campaign Craft: The Strategies, Tactics, and Art of Political Campaign Management* (Westport, CT: Praeger, 3rd ed., 2006), 10-11.

14 Shea and Burton, 12

15 The National Council of State Legislatures compiles these figures every two years. In 2015-16, 260 of (48.6%) members of Congress had served previously in a state legislature.

16 The more highly educated the voters, the more likely they are to respond. One of the problems in 2016 was the failure of many polls to control for this by increasing or overweighting the responses of less educated voters (who were considerably more likely to vote for Trump). The education gap in 2016 was unusually strong which is probably why so many pollsters failed to take it into account. See Nate Cohen, "A 2016 Review: Why Key State Polls Were Wrong About Trump," *The New York Times,* May 31, 2017, A25.

17 On these forms of what they call "actualizing citizenship" see W. Lance Bennett, Deen Freelon and Chris Wells, "Changing Citizen Identity and the Rise of a Participatory Media Culture," in Lonnie R. Sherrod, Judith Torney-Purta and Constance A Flanagan, *Handbook of Research on Civic Engagement in Youth* (Hoboken, NJ: John Wiley and Sons, 2010), 393-423.

18 Pippa Norris, "The Evolution of Election Campaigns: Eroding Political Engagement?" paper published by the Harvard University School of Government, January 17, 2004, available at hks.Harvard.edu/fs/pnorris/Acrobat/Otago/The/Evolution/ of/Election/Campaigns.pdf, p. 7.

19 Daniel Kreiss, *Prototype Politics: Technology-Intensive Campaigning and the Data of Democracy* (New York: Oxford University Press, 2016), 219.

20 Theda Skocpol, *The Missing Middle: Working Families and the Future of American Social Policy* (New York: The Century Foundation, 2000), 167.i

21 Daniel Kreiss, *Taking Our Country Back: The Crafting of Networked Politics from Howard Dean to Barak Obama* (New York: Oxford University Press, 2012), 23.

22 Quoted in ibid. 27.

23 See Robert K. Merton's classic essay, "The Latent Functions of the Machine: A Sociologist's View," in Merton, *Social Theory and Social Structure* (Glencoe, IL: The Free Press, 1957), 75. This classic essay, together with a rich assortment of cases studies and analytic essays can be found in Alexander B. Callow, Jr., *The City Boss in America: An Interpretive Reader* (New York: Oxford University Press, 1976). Arguably the best, and certainly the most fun to read, of the many case studies of individual machines is Milton Rakove, *Don't Make No Waves. . . Don't Back No Losers: An Insiders' Analysis of the Daley Machine* (Bloomington: Indiana University Press, 1976).

24 Frank R. Kent, *The Great Game of Politics* (Garden City, NY: Doubleday, Doran and Co., 1933), 11.

25 Ibid. 10.

26 A handful of states have open primary laws that allow voters to cast ballots in the contests of parties in which they are not enrolled; but in most states you must be registered with a party to vote in its primary.

27 Edward V. Schneier, John Brian Murtaugh and Antoinette Pole, *New York Politics: A Tale of Two States* (Armonk, NY: M, E. Sharper, 2010), 74.

28 Kent, 10.

29 Ibid. 11.

30 Marjorie Randon Hershey, *Party Politics in America* (New York: Routledge, 2016), 90.

31 Kreiss, 16.

32 Thomas E. Mann and Norman J. Ornstein, *The Broken Branch* (New York: Oxford University Press, 2006) and *It's Even Worse than It Looks* (New York: Basic Books, 2012).

33   Woodrow Wilson, *Congressional Government* (New York: Meridian Books, 1956; originally published in 1885), 31.

34   Committee on Political Parties, American Political Science Association, "Toward a More Responsible Two-Party System," 44 *American Political Science Review* (March, 1950), 1-14.

35   For a full account of these reforms see Nelson W. Polsby, *How Congress Evolves: Social Bases of Institutional Change* (New York: Oxford University Press, 2004).

36   The phrase is from Richard Fenno's path-breaking study of the Appropriations Committees. Richard F. Fenno, Jr., *The Power of the Purse: Appropriations Politics in Congress* (Boston: Little, Brown and Company, 1966).

37   Theodore J. Lowi, *The End of Liberalism: The Second Republic of the United States* (New York: W. W. Norton, 2nd ed., 1979), xiii.

38   Eric S. Heberling and Bruce A. Larson, *Congressional Parties, Institutional Ambition, and the Financing of Majority Control* (Ann Arbor: The University of Michigan Press, 2012), 262.

39   William Bendix, "Bypassing Congressional Committees: Parties, Panel Rosters, and Deliberative Processes," 45 *Legislative Studies Quarterly* (August 2016), 690

40   Ibid. 77.

41   William F. Connelly, Jr., John J. Pitney, Jr., and Gary J. Schmitt, eds., *Is Congress Broken? The Virtues and Defects of Partisanship and Gridlock* (Washington: Brookings Institution Press, 2017), 180.

42   Marc J. Hetherington and Thomas J. Rudolph, *Why Washington Won't Work* (Chicago: University of Chicago Press, 2015), 15.

43   Ibid. 38.

44   John Kenneth White and Jerome M. Mileur, "In the Spirit of Their Times: 'Toward a More Responsible Two-Party System' and Party Politics," in John C. Green and Paul S. Herrnson, *Responsible Partisanship: The Evolution of American Political Parties since 1950* (Lawrence: University Press of Kansas, 2002), 33.

45 Reuven Y. Hazan, ed., *Cohesion and Discipline in Legislatures: Political Parties, Parliamentary Committees, Party Leadership and Governance* (London: Taylor and Francis, 2006).

46 Phillip J. Cooper, *By Order of the President: The Use and Abuse of Executive Direct Action* (Lawrence: University Press of Kansas, 2002), 242.

Chapter 2

Putting People Back in Politics

Executive Summary and Action Guide

Although the President's party generally loses votes in off-years, Democrats will have an unusually hard time winning control of the House and even less in the Senate; but the 2018 elections are of vital importance in narrowing the Republican majority, changing state legislatures, setting the stage for 2020 and creating a new Democratic Party directed from the grassroots up.

It is never too early to start registering new voters and canvassing neighborhoods. For those who don't live in competitive districts (see the appendices for a preliminary list), many people have second homes or close relatives and friends that are in districts that can be flipped in 2018. Even for those in one-party areas, it may still be worthwhile to consider becoming a party official. It's not hard, and party building may pay off in 2020 and in the longer run. Most party organizations welcome volunteers, but you may need to look for reform groups or even work with friends and neighbors to start the process.

The first step for a volunteer, or for a candidate, is to map the district. The elaborate files of the party's national committees— the absolute best starting point— are generally not available to non-incumbents or until candidates have been chosen. But a basic map of where the parties are strongest, where turnout varies, and where swing voters are most common is easily constructed from figures available from the Board of Elections. Basic demographic data can be found in the census, and a variety of political websites, such as the Cook and Rothenberg Reports, Larry Sabato, Ballotpedia, Roll Call and Politico offer both past election returns and updates on competitive districts.

Starting with these maps the starting point is to build a data base, register voters and recruit volunteers. Equally important, in an early canvas is its role in providing links between candidates, parties and voters. Volunteers cannot always tell people how to get food stamps or social security, they can put them in touch with people who do. And they can get people to provide feedback not always found in polls. Again, it is never too early to stake out a neighborhood and get to know its voters.

Some basic knowledge of election laws is essential, especially as to filing deadlines, registration rules, caucus and petitioning rules and deadlines (in some states). One of the reasons organization is important is to make sure these jobs get done. If party organizations are weak, it may be necessary to form mechanisms for working within and across the political boundaries of state, local and national district lines. Every election cycle reams of volunteer-generated data and information are unnecessarily lost the day after the election. It is not easy. Many Americans will never will know their neighbors, and among those who do, conversations that range beyond the weather and work are limited; about politics, rarer still. Properly used, the internet can ease the social costs of these interactions, but getting people back into politics in an authentic sense involves the "difficult" process of A actually talking to B.

The four steps that must be taken to change the political landscape are: first, to join, form, revitalize, or take over the local party committee; second, to research the district and its politicians; third, to hit the road to talk with, register, and persuade actual voters; and fourth, looping back to the first, to provide an institutional foundation that treats each election as an episode in a long campaign rather than an isolated event. For those averse to going door to door, there is work to be done; but the whole thesis of this book is that the surest and most cost-effective way to make a difference is through face-to-face communication. The 2018 elections are important in their own right; they also need to serve as a fulcrum for the levers of long-term change in the balance of political power and in the way we conduct elections. The campaign professionals who dominate campaigns have important roles to play, so does the money that pays for them; but unless and until both candidates and voters are reconnected, and unless and until the grassroots forces of progressive politics are revitalized, the real impact of the Congress elected in a single off-year election will be more symbolic than substantive.

1. What Is at Stake in 2018?

The 2018 elections will serve both as indicators of interest in changing the Congress and as harbingers of presidential politics in 2020. While the party out of power generally makes significant gains in off year elections (when the presidency is not on the ballot), Democrats would need to win twenty-four House seats to gain a majority. They face an even more difficult task in the Senate where only eight of thirty-three seats in play are currently held by Republicans. Five of the Democrats who must run in 2018, moreover, are from states that Trump carried by more than 20% in 2016.

Even if progressive candidates cannot gain control of the House or Senate, politicians and pundits will sift through the ballots to see if they can find a mandate for change, or portents for 2020. And a good showing by Democrats might at least slow the reactionary legislative agenda. Members of Congress who win with sixty percent of the vote are generally less attentive to opposition viewpoints than those win by small majorities. It will also make a difference if the vanishing species of responsible Republicans can survive hard right primary challenges. With reapportionment on every state's agenda in 2021, moreover, partisan control of state legislatures is increasingly important. Every legislative district, state and national must be redrawn in 2021. More is at stake in 2018, in other words, then numerical control of the House and Senate in 2019. Particularly in the wake of Trump's surprise victory in 2016, the symbolic impact on the calculations of candidates looking toward 2020, and the perceptions of campaign contributors, volunteers and ordinary voters that will be structured in large part by the outcome of 2018's House, Senate and state elections.

The good news is that it is in the nature of midterm elections to enhance the importance of volunteers. Whether direct contact can change the minds of voters is not clear, what it most certainly can do is register new voters, increase voter turnout and enhance and refine the data bases that will fuel future campaigns.

The historic drop-off in turnout between presidential and off-years ranges from as little as twelve percent to more than twenty. The fall-off is generally higher among voters of the party of the incumbent President. This so-called "presidential penalty" arises out of the stronger negative feelings of out-party members and a seeming desire on the part of voters to balance party control in the government. The popularity of the President in power is a key factor, quite obviously, because congressional members of his or her party are– justifiably or not– held accountable for his or her problems. Of equal importance in the fact that the weaker the party in power seems to be, the more likely it is that electable opponents will decide to run.

Especially given the poor ratings voters have been giving the Trump administration, the 2018 picture is not as rosy for the Democrats as it might seem. "What happens," as Nathan Gonzalez of *Roll Call* asked, "When voters perceive the president to be outside the traditional two-party system? Trump is technically a Republican because he ascended though the GOP nominating process. Still, many voters see him as his own brand rather than as a party leader. If that differentiation continues, GOP candidates could avoid the typical midterm disaster."[1] It may also be that Republicans suffer fewer midterm losses than Democrats. While Latinos and African Americans, poor and less educated citizens, and self-professed independents have low off-year turnout rates, the differences between these groups and other voters are pretty much the same as they are in presidential election years. But fall-offs in turnout are sharp among young voters and self-described liberals.[2] Because older voters and conservatives are less likely to stay at home in off-years, in other words, younger and more liberal voters need to be especially motivated if the usual midterm politics of surge and decline take hold. It goes without saying that the Democrat's ability to recruit candidates with particular appeal to these groups is important. And because younger liberals are the voters most associated with support for Bernie Sanders, it will be more important than ever for Democrats to avoid the kinds of sharply divisive primaries that produce wounds that carry over into November. Fortunately for Democrats, there is growing evidence that the degree of intra-party polarization is growing faster in the Republican Party than among Democrats.[3] Beyond the split between Tea Party supporters and more mainstream types, there would also seem to being growing divisions in support for President Trump. It is likely that we will see a significant number of incumbent Republicans challenged in primaries in 2018, some successfully. While it is increasingly clear that many of Trump's most ardent supporters are very much at odds with so-called establishment Republicans, the key question is whether and how much these divisions will effect general election outcomes. Whether, for example, Arizona Republicans, without retiring Senator Jeff Flake on the ballot, can reunify the party sufficiently to win in November is as much up in the air, as is the question of whether continuing clashes between the Clinton and Sanders wings of the Democratic Party can work together. One interesting study of campaign giving provides a possibly telling indicator. Looking at Federal Election Commission reports Blum, Koch and Podkul found that campaign donors to unsuccessful Republican primary candidates were significantly less likely to contribute to the ultimate general election candidates than were the supporters of unsuccessful Democratic challengers.[4]

Both parties' national committees and congressional campaign committees have become increasingly active in recruiting candidates. Many state committees have become similarly involved. While these efforts generally come with the promise of substantial financial and professional help, they are not always sensitive to local issues and personalities. And they are not particularly likely to seek out candidates who appeal to younger voters or who are significantly more liberal. This is why local organizations are so much needed. Not only must regional factors be taken into account in recruiting candidates, but campaigns run along cookie-cutter national models are even less likely to be effective in off-years. Campaigns run from outside of the district bind them into patterns of activity and methods of campaigning that, as argued in Chapter 1 are increasingly less effective and possibly counterproductive. Cases in point, the four by-elections in 2017 to replace retiring Republican members of the House. Here are the districts, the amounts reportedly contributed by the Democratic national committees to each, the final margins of loss, and the differences in the losing margins between 2016 and 2017:

District	Amount Spent	2017 Losing Margin	Democratic Improvement From 2016 to 2017
Georgia 5	$5,000,000	3.8%	+ 19.4
South Carolina 5	275,000	3.2%	+ 17.1
Montana AL	200,000	6.1%	+ 10.4
Kansas 4	no significant funds	6.8%	+ 23.9

The largest increase was in Kansas, where national party help was virtually non-existent, and the closest race was in South Carolina, where the national effort was rather small. While no definitive conclusions can be drawn from this limited set of cases, the party's maximum effort in Georgia was not decisively superior. Some of the reasons for this are rather obvious. Although Republican and independent expenditures were not as great as those of the Democrats, they were substantial, helping make this election in the most expensive in history. And the Democratic candidate, unlike his Republican opponent was a political novice who did not actually live in the district.

Whatever else it shows, the Georgia race is clearly illustrative of the fact that even a massive national effort cannot produce victory and, indeed, may not even help at all. Tip O'Neill's famous maxim that "all politics is local" continues to resonate. There is strong anecdotal evidence, on social media and in the press, moreover, that many voters in Georgia both resented being targets of outside influence and overwhelmed to the point of nausea with the bombardment of ads, flyers and strangers at their doors. And the bottom line quite simply is that is that although Democrats raised and spent a great deal more money in this race than did the Republicans, this case is exceptional in that the Republicans thought the seat was safe. In the long run the big bucks go the other way, and the independent expenditures of business and conservative will always more than match those of progressives.

Party loyalties have hardened, but there remain large blocs of voters who can be influenced. And the highly sophisticated national model of polling, targeted ads, robo calls and paid canvassing is not working very well. The very real question is whether today's reform political activists have the stamina to create a new politics of reform. There are useful historical precedents. In California, in the 1950s, a system known as cross-filing allowed anyone of either party to run in the other party's primary. My friend, Steve Zetterburg ran against a young, well-funded congressman, Richard Nixon. Because parties were not allowed to make primary endorsements, the Nixon campaign saturated the district with billboards with no party affiliation mentioned. Every night, Zetterburg's volunteers posted a strip saying "Republican" between the lines "Vote for Richard Nixon" and "for Congress," and every morning Republican volunteers would paste a plain strip of paper blocking it out it. By primary day the billboards were an inch thick and Nixon won both the Democratic and Republican lines.

Reform Democrats in California went around this system by forming local "clubs" able to make primary endorsements. The clubs soon coalesced into the California Democratic Council of Clubs (CDC) that began to recruit and endorse on a statewide level. Similarly, in New York, the success of reform Democrats in replacing Tammany leader Carmine DeSapio led to the organization of a New Democratic Coalition of Clubs (NDC) that became a major player, particularly in the city. The CDC, NDC and similar groups such as the Independent Voters of Illinois remained influential throughout the 1970s, and still have some local pockets of power. The rise and fall of the club movement illustrates both the potentials and problems of reform politics. They were, in the immortal words of Tammany's Boss Plunkitt, "mornin' glories– looked lovely in the mornin' and withered up in a short time."[5] In a very real sense, the club movement was the victim of its own success: once elected with club help, incumbent politicians grew increasingly wary of being too closely associated with the sometimes "radical" clubs.

Reform comes in cycles: we elect a Pat Brown, a Mario Cuomo, a number of thoughtful, progressive members of the House and Senate, and . . . the organizational imperative fades. How to build and sustain a movement for real change is the dominant issue of 2018. What such a movement needs to succeed beyond the election is the kind of institutional memory that organizations like the CDC provided. The CDC analogy is particularly relevant because the California clubs– instead of forming in reaction to entrenched machines as in New York and Illinois– were filling a void, which is the situation faced by most reform Democrats today. In most areas, in fact, what is left of the regular organizations will probably join happily into a movement to revive the party. A new machine, created and directed from the grassroots up instead of top down, can do for progressives what Tammany did for immigrants.

A major shortcoming of the club movement was that virtually all of its organizing energy was generated in relatively affluent communities often in neighborhoods that were largely Republican. Through the statewide Council of Clubs in California and the state Democratic Coalition in New York, the reformers could be a significant factor in statewide Democratic primaries, in local races, and in more affluent, liberal areas like Hollywood or university towns like Berkeley, California and the Hyde Park area in Chicago. But because it had almost no footing in the working class and minority neighborhoods where Democrats were strongest in general elections, its fortunes were mixed. New York's NDC many old-timers suggested actually stood for "November Don't Count." It was, in a sense a bad rap: in Pat Brown's victory over Richard Nixon for Governor of California, in Mario Cuomo's election as Governor of New York, and in numerous races for local office, the reformers of the 1970s and 80s were highly effective in forming alliances with regular organization Democrats in Black and Latino areas, but it remains a cautionary tale.

Such alliances can be formed and sustained. In Brooklyn, New York, for example, two activists mobilized by Barak Obama's 2008 campaign approached the head of the King's county Democratic organization to join the county committee and were basically told, "Do not do this, do not run for county committee, just volunteer." Forming a New Kings movement, the activists found that they could not only win seats on the committee, but that in many cases– due to vacancies– all they had to do was file. There is still friction within the county organization, and the old-timers are still in charge, but the dynamic has changed.[6] The New

Kings have morphed from pariahs to players. Gaining access to, or taking over a previously impermeable organization will probably produce better public officials. But significant battles to change the direction of American politics in 2018 will not, by and large, be fought in Brooklyn. What are the alternatives– beyond clicking on a box in your e-mail to send a few dollars to a candidate in Podunk– for people who live in one of the roughly 350 House districts or twenty-odd states that are pretty much safe for one party or the other?

At least four percent of Americans own more than one home. Factor in students at residential colleges, and those who live in one place but frequently overnight in another, and there are probably more than ten percent of us who legitimately can claim voting residence in more than one place. (Correction: you *cannot* register or vote in more than one place, that's a felony; but you can register in the one of your choice.) Check the politics, register in a place with more competitive districts. Having some tie to a place is an enormous asset in going door-to-door. It's not just knowing the neighborhood but the simple difference between saying, "Hi, I live down the street and want to talk to you about the upcoming election". . . and "Hi, I want to talk to you about the upcoming election;" and it's the difference between flying blind and knowing what kinds of issues are likely to be on voters' minds. The next best thing to having a second residence is having a relative in one: if, for example, you live in a Chicago district that is ninety percent Democratic, but your daughter and son-in-law are in the west Chicago suburbs, where the districts are more competitive, you might spend some door-to-door time there (preferably with one of your relatives).

2. Mapping the District

One of the key problems with candidate-centered campaigns was the need to keep reinventing the wheel. When a candidate ran a decent but losing campaign against an incumbent, his or her organization tended to fade back into the woodwork. The next challenger was forced, essentially, to start all over putting together a campaign team, finding donors, taking polls, organizing local committees and community contacts, developing registration and a get-out-the vote drives, connecting with local governments and organizations. Ongoing organizations can perform most of these functions.

The national committees of both parties, as we noted in chapter one, have become increasingly sophisticated in doing much of the groundwork for these efforts. The Democrat's VoteBuilder program "extended the ability of the party and its candidates to contest elections and to target the electorate. It enabled Democratic candidates for office from state senator to president to share data across campaigns and election cycles, while ensuring that the voter rile was continuously updated with quality data."[7] The question of who should have access to this resource has yet to be fully resolved. In 2016, some tech savvy members of Bernie Sander's campaign managed to hack Hillary Clinton's customized data files, resulting in the DNC's suspending Sander's use of the VoteBuilder system. The issue was resolved within twenty four hours, but it highlighted what is almost certain to be an ongoing controversy.

Currently, the national committees control access to these files for presidential campaigns, carefully firewalling each candidates' particular uses of the data. Fifty state parties, plus the District of Columbia's control access for their own campaigns. Obviously, the chances are good that this results in a tilt toward incumbents, with some states explicitly denying access to challengers. Even more controversial is the possibility that the efforts of the national committees and of the Senate and House campaign committees– which are growing increasingly active in candidate recruitment– will use access to these data bases to over-ride the preferences of local party groups. At the same time, there are eighteen states that do not hold their congressional primaries until August or September, leaving an impossibly short time in which to organize a campaign. Particularly for those challenging incumbent Republicans, it is absolutely vital to be fully in the field far earlier. There may be cases, moreover, in which one of more of the Democrats running in the primary could prove something of an embarrassment if he or she won. It is for these reasons that Daniel Kreiss, who has probably explored these issues as closely as anyone, argues that as long as the process of access is fair, these files are "a distinctively *partisan* resource," and should be evaluated as such.

> In essence, the Democratic Party has created a powerful and robust tool that facilitates its efforts to secure political power. And, I believe, in keeping with the normative role of parties in democratic societies, the party should have control access to it according to their own policies designed to further their governance interests. As a matter of course, these policies and remedies should be

> transparent and ultimately contestable . . .
> but in the end . . . it is a good thing that
> as a multi-issue coalition of heterogeneous
> actors the Democratic Party sets its own
> policies and procedures for its use as a
> database.[8]

The caveats to this position pertain both to transparency and contestability and whether the folks in Washington can keep their thumbs off the scale. Although logic suggests that if they want to win as many races as possible, the national parties would not willfully over-ride the clear preferences of local party activists, but logic and politics do not always coincide. Leaving it to the state parties to decide— as is the case in New York— is probably the best compromise.

Given fair and full access, these data bases provide an incredibly rich starting point for local activists. The dream of national leaders "to create whole citizens in data," or "to use digital observational technologies and databases developed over the past two decades to reveal and leverage the psychological dispositions and social lives of citizens for electoral purposes"[9] is not yet a reality, and it is not at all certain that it should be. Having people in place throughout a district, however, who are armed with data identifying hard core supporters, opponents and neutrals, is not unrealistic at all. Indeed it is how future election campaigns can be both more effective and democratic, and how we can make politics up close and personal once again. Unlike electronic data bases running on their own, local groups using these files can help repersonalize the contacts between voters and elected politicians. Local activists, who can treat individuals as whole people rather than entries on a digital map, like the old precinct captains of the machine age, are the key to this kind of "new" politics. What the computer models misses are the interactive processes that made the old machines work: you canvas not just to sell your candidates or get out the vote, but to connect your citizens to their polity. In the narrowest sense, the point of going door-to-door is to build a data base, register new voters and get your supporters to the polls. More importantly it is to connect people with their government. You, as a volunteer, may not know about how to connect with social security or apply for a student or small business loan; but the point of organization is to link people with experts who can answer these questions. An effective political club can go beyond getting out the vote in a single election to developing both an actual and virtual map of the district.

The average population of a congressional district, based on the 2010 census was close to 650,000, it is now closer to 740,000. Some, heavy in non-citizens– who count for apportionment but cannot vote– have far fewer potential voters; others, with rapidly growing populations have far more. Volunteers can only reach so many people, and polls as we have noted, have often reached the point at which surveys of, say, Hispanics or rural voters become prohibitively expensive. What the national committee's increasingly sophisticated systems can do is to locate where previous party candidates have done well, where swing voters are most commonly found, where turnout is problem, and so on; and then, more importantly, link this data to polls and canvassing data that provide demographic correlatives. As Kreiss puts it,

Contemporary campaigning is not so much an embodied or organization-based practice on the order of Tammany, as an attempt to use digital observational technologies and databases developed over the two decades to reveal and leverage the psychological dispositions and social lives of citizens for electoral purposes. To leverage these tools, however, requires combining and integrating data stores that offer only partial fragmented views of individuals.[10]

It also requires a real sense of these individuals as citizens, as real people with political ideas, needs and issue concerns. Effective campaigning is in part about techniques, psychological dispositions, the targeting key groups and demographic analyses; but it also about representation and a continuing dialogue between politicians and their constituents about public policy. At the same time, an effective campaign does not treat all citizens equally. When you pick cherries, as campaign consultant Matt Reese was fond of saying, you start where cherries grow. Political maps begin with data from past elections. Given a finite source of volunteers the first place to look for progressive (or conservative) votes in areas that have voted for progressive (or conservative) candidates in the past.

What the newer data bases provide is the ability to move beyond geographic maps to infinitely more sophisticated maps of individual voters in whatever their fixed abodes. The traditional mapping of a district also involves working through existing groups from labor unions to rotary clubs and local businesses. Many large organizations host candidates' nights, unavoidable even if they seldom produce new supporters, but less formal events– at lunch breaks in factories, at regular meetings of clubs, at their fund-raising events– provide opportunities to go one-on-one, meeting people on their own turf. And groups can, in a sense, be created. "Big Jim" Folsom, arguably Alabama's most progressive Governor, would drive into a small town, go to the local general store to buy lunch, a snack or a cup of coffee and talk with owner, then sit down inside or out on the sidewalk to talk politics with anyone who came along. Those were simpler days, and even in rural areas walking into the Dollar Store is not quite the same as the general store of Alabama sixty years ago; but local volunteers can almost always point candidates to local establishments– a local library or church, senior home, garden store or hairdresser– that has the pulse of some segment of the community. It's an educational opportunity for the candidate, and while it may not earn many direct votes it helps establish a needed buzz. With computers, more importantly, all of the data collected in these encounters can be plugged into the district map.

In 1979, Richard Fenno suggested that "the more fragmented and kinetic American society becomes, the more difficult it will be for House members to reach people."[11] Even then, no matter how he or she allocates time, it is possible to reach "a relatively few people directly." Rightly or wrongly, however, all of the candidates Fenno followed in his landmark study, believed, "That as a result of their direct contact with as many supportive constituencies as they can reach, they will also reach a great many more people indirectly. They are great believers in the two-step flow of communications. They have to be. But they also think that it works."[12] As with Big Jim Folsom, it wasn't so much the people who sat with him on the sidewalk, but those who weren't there but heard that he had been. It is a form of advertising that is made the more effective by its interactive nature. The key to rebuilding the Democratic Party is to cumulate every one of these encounters into the data base, to develop a person by person map of every town and district that informs every ensuing campaign.

For better or worse, it is amazing– if not a bit frightening– how far along we are in actually developing such maps. At a recent conference on the uses of e-mail, one of the participants told of using his smart phone in Washington to locate a Walgreen's pharmacy on his way to the airport. Delayed by traffic he went directly to his flight. When he arrived in New York, his phone told him, without prompting, where could find Walgreens in New York. The sheer amount of data available combined with the political algorithms that can with increasing accuracy "predict" the political preferences of both populations and individuals is beyond most people's comprehension. Armed with such data, the doyens of this technology argue, all that remains for volunteers is to converse and connect with the actual human beings the computers have mapped.

3. Organizing for Victory

Let's get real here. First of all, the computers aren't all that good. Nor will you ever find enough volunteers to the kind of voter contact operations needed to win in marginal districts. A lot of ardent, political people are simply uncomfortable going door-to-door or contacting strangers by phone. And many of the areas where turnout is lowest, and where canvassing might do the most good, volunteers are scarce. Neighborhoods with large immigrant populations, both legal and eligible to vote and illegal and not eligible, are careful about opening the door to strangers. Yet these are the areas in which progressive candidates tend to do best, but where turnout is most problematic in general, and most likely to fall off in midterm elections. In the 2017 special congressional election in Georgia, the Democrats would almost certainly have won if as many African-American voters turned out as in 2016. There is no organizational challenge more important to the Democratic Party, yet less close to a solution than that of broadening its volunteer and voter base in minority areas. It is ironic that the party most generally supportive of affirmative action in principle has given so little attention to it practice. One solution, that is really not that difficult, is to pay people to go door-to-door in their own neighborhoods. While it may raise distasteful memories of the old political machines, part-time jobs registering voters and getting them to the polls, involving citizens in campaigns who could not otherwise afford the time, and, coincidentally of course, helping the campaign cannot be all bad.

Although language barriers pose a clear problem in some ethnic enclaves, experiments have shown that it is not at all clear that "canvassers who 'match' the ethnic profile of the neighborhood tend to have more success than those who do not."[13] There is, however, considerable evidence that those who have local ties to the area are more effective than outsiders.[14] It would seem to follow that an organizational sensitivity to neighborhood concerns is worth developing and, hopefully, sustained over time either by strengthening the formal party structure or creating a parallel system of clubs. Real change requires real work, and in politics there is no substitute for organization. Absent the levers of patronage, pelf and political ambition that sustained the old machines, the challenge today is that of sustaining the policy-focused enthusiasm of reformers. Annual or twice-a-year reports from elected officials both help them keep in touch and increase interest in the club. In states with referenda, bringing in experts to explain their effects; meetings on college admissions, social security and various local issues; purely social events, and the usual things that voluntary organizations do can help. In the heyday of New York City's Village Independent Democrats, there were people who looked forward as much to the post-meeting beers at the Lion's Head as to the meetings themselves.

Two small caveats are in order here. The core purpose of a political organization is to win elections, not to hold fund-raisers and social events and protect their own party positions. The withering of organizations begins when they focus more on protecting themselves than they do on elections. All too often, party organizations spend more effort fending off primary challenges to their county and state committee members than they do in welcoming new members In state after state in 2016, Democratic organizations, instead of welcoming the energized supporters of Bernie Sanders, treated them as if they were enemies. Many Sander's supporters, in turn, responded by acting as if Hillary Clinton and the so-called party establishment was a greater enemy than Donald Trump.

A related problem with most organizations stems from what the German sociologist Robert Michels called the "iron law of oligarchy." Disturbed that Europe's social democratic parties, despite their strong verbal support for democracy, were in their own internal governance all but immune to internal challenges, Michels suggested that parties and other membership organizations were almost invariably doomed to oligarchy. Once a leadership team is in place, efficiency demands the kind of specialized division of labor found in bureaucracies; and as an organization becomes bureuacratized the gap between the skills of leaders and the rank and file becomes virtually unbreachable. To be successful, parties need professionals on top. Once on top, those same professionals control the mailing lists, the meeting agendas, and files that give them virtual immunity to challenge.[15] This same dynamic, as it increasingly alienates the rank and file, may in the long run contain the seeds of its own destruction. This, in a way, was the fate of Tammany: the more tightly its leadership resisted internal dissent, the more the pressure for change expanded until it exploded in the form challenging institutions like the reform clubs that defeated Carmine DeSapio. Bureaucratic parties similarly run the risk of simply fading away. Long out of touch with a changing electorate, they become at once so secure yet so remote in their offices that they no longer know how to win a fight. The best cure for this kind of problem begins with awareness and goes to conscious and recurring drives to bring in new members, recruit new leaders and avoid putting too much responsibility in the hands of too few people.

4. Getting Started

The first step in political organizing is to locate yourself politically, which is not as easy as it sounds. Most Americans elect at least one set of local officials who govern a defined town, city, borough or whatever; county or parish governments cover a wider jurisdiction in most states; 49 of the fifty states elect governors and two houses of the legislature (Nebraska has a one-house legislature), and— in most states— other statewide officials such as Attorneys General, Lieutenant Governors, Secretaries of State, Commissioners of Agriculture, and so on. Judges, sheriffs and magistrates, if elected rather than appointed, may run at the town, county or state level, or from special judicial districts. School boards are elected in most states from districts that often cross town and county lines. Villages, boroughs, parishes, cities and townships sometimes overlap with, or surround other local governments; and most states have at least a few elected special districts for water, fire, irrigation, flood control, street lights or libraries. For those who focus on national issues, these congruent, separate and overlapping jurisdictions often involve wading into uncharted waters where, they sometimes find, those who were their staunchest allies on big national issues have very different priorities when it comes to local, legal or educational issues.

Following Robert Merton, sociologists often distinguish between what are called "cosmopolitans" and "locals," orientations that are not mutually exclusive but define broad tendencies that sometimes vex political organizations. The more local the race the more partisanship and ideology take a back seat to personality and accessibility. And the more you move away from general governing bodies– whether local, state or national– to special agencies like library boards, fire and water districts, and boards of education, the more important it is to keep them in rooms of their own. The issues that divide people in school politics do not generally coincide closely with those that divide people in state, local or national elections.

In the days of the machine, straight-ticket voting was common. It declined in the 1960s, 70s and 80s, replaced by what political scientists called candidate-centered-campaigns. A popular book at the time, *The Party's Over*, by the respected journalist David Broder, argued, as its title suggests that party organizations were becoming increasingly irrelevant, pushed aside by self-starting (usually wealthy) interest groups and political action committees.[16] But as party lines have tightened, it seems as if fewer voters, especially at the national level, are voting for individuals rather than parties. Indeed the 2016 elections were the first in modern history in which every state elected a senator of the same party as its presidential choice. Party organizations– from the national committees down to the local level– are playing a more important role in nominations, campaigns and fund-raising.

What this indicates in specific terms for 2018 is not obvious. It is not certain that the unpopularity of the president will affect the vote for the House and Senate, much less if for state and local offices. But the massive incompetence thus far displayed by the party controlling both houses of congress and the White House is a leverage issue just waiting to be exploited. One telling indicator of Republican problems is found in the number and quality of candidates prepared to run against incumbent members of the House and Senate. As a general rule, incumbents who run for re-election win. Since 1974, the re-election rate for House incumbents has dipped below 90% only twice (in 1992, 88% and 2010, 85%). Senators, with six year terms, are only slightly more vulnerable, with more than 80% typically getting reelected. These numbers become less daunting in times of political flux. One of the reasons incumbents usually win is because they do, making it unlikely for quality challengers to take them on. When the incumbent president's poll numbers are low, however, or the economy floundering, the possibility of beating an incumbent increases along with the hopes of potential challengers.

This can pose a somewhat unusual problem for activists. Instead of trying to find someone willing to run, many congressional districts already have lines of potential candidates. Particularly in rural and some suburban districts, congressional districts encompass numerous counties or assembly districts that define the jurisdictions of party organizations. There are few mechanisms through which these diverse constituencies can cooperate. Smelling blood in the water, there are districts in mid-2017 in which more than half a dozen candidates had already announced their 2018 candidacies. There is a large library of studies of the effects of divisive primaries. The conclusions are essentially opaque in part because there is no good way statistically to measure just *how* divisive the primary is, but it does seem that the higher the visibility of the race the more negative the effects. Fouirnaies and Hall, for example, found a substantial negative effect on the general election for House and Senate candidates, but almost none for state legislatures.[17] Some previous studies have suggested that divisive primaries can sometimes give a bounce to the winning candidate, largely by increasing name recognition; but Fouirnaires and Hall make a convincing case for largely negative effects. Primaries, moreover, sap money and volunteer energies that detract from the November election effort.

As desirable as it is to winnow the list and hopefully avoid a divisive primary, the problems at the congressional level are particularly difficult. Parties are typically organized by town, county, ward or assembly district lines that seldom coincide with congressional districts. State party organizations are the go-to bodies for Senate races and state-wide races like governor and attorney general, but for the House of Representatives, the mechanisms for bringing local organizations together are virtually non-existent, especially for challengers. House incumbents, have already organized a winning campaign, and have the added advantage of two years of experience in serving all parts of the district. For challengers and in open-seat districts, the sooner local groups reach out to each other and develop cooperative relations the better their chances. In some areas, groups coming out of local parties and organizations like Indivisible have actually begun raising general election money for whatever Democrat wins the primary. In other districts, local party leaders have set up inter-community screening panels to endorse a consensus candidate in advance of the primary.

The nasty fact remains, however, that more than four out of five American live in districts where the chances of beating incumbents are little better than of winning the lottery. You can play for fun and, in fact, there are good reasons to organize in non-competitive areas, but to be most effective in 2018 you should look at the lists presented in the Appendices to leverage your efforts. Some districts and states where there seems no hope may not be as hopeless as they seem. One will seldom have an opportunity like Democrats were given in the Alabama Senate election in 2017 of running against an already weak candidate credibly accused of deviance; and although such cases are rare, off year primary elections in seemingly safe seats can, with low turnout, allow the nuts in the Republican Party to take over the asylum and nominate one of their own.

Similar bad choices at the national level can resonate widely as in 1964 when the nomination of Barry Goldwater enabled Democrats to win literally dozens of House and Senate seats normally considered solidly Republican. Whether Trump's extraordinarily low poll numbers, as we have suggested elsewhere, will be similarly resonant is hard to say. But what makes the 1964 case particularly interesting is that many of those Democrats who upset incumbents in seemingly solid Republican districts were able to hold on to their seats in 1966 and beyond. The explanation is part, is that many of the long-term Republicans who lost in 1964 had lost touch with their districts. They lost, not only because of Goldwater but because they had never really been tested; and when new, vigorous Democrats came in and were seen as responsive to their constituents as their predecessors had not, a message was sent. In solidly Democratic districts, conversely, it seems likely— for similar reasons— there are likely to be incumbents who can be beaten in primaries or at least changed by effective opposition. We will look at the problem of candidate recruitment more extensively in chapter three.

One final note. Even in, or especially in, districts firmly in control of one party or the other, the party organizations in those districts will have substantial influence over who will be selected as the delegates to the 2020 National Convention. Rather than complain later about the system being stacked, the time to get involved is now.

5. An Agenda for Action

Although it is never too early for activists to begin the hunt for new voters, most campaigns don't really get under way publicly until late spring (depending of course on whether and when a party primary may be called for). But an effective campaign begins long before that. The first step is to become familiar with the state's election calendar and the deadlines for voter registration and such necessary tasks as filing for candidacy, holding caucuses (in some states), filing petitions, and reporting on campaign finances. It is also important to check on various state and local laws relating to campaigns: two of my friends in California spent an afternoon in jail for violating a noise ordinance in a town where I had sent them with a sound truck. They didn't think it was funny. Nor would your candidate find it funny if fined for putting up lawn signs in a town that prohibits them more than thirty days before an election. This is one of the reasons organization is so important: where there is viable party or club that there are people who know how to do these things. If there is a competitive primary each of the candidates will have their own organizations that– if they are viable– will in effect train a number of volunteers for the fall general election.

If an organization in your area has yet to coalesce, there are simple ways of acting on your own. Your local Board of Elections has lists (often accessible on line), generally sorted by party, that provide a starting point. Usually you can get what is called a walking list that identifies registered voters in numerical street order, so if you walk down Elm Street and see that there are registered voters in numbers 17 and 19, but none at 18, try to sign them up. And check to see that all the over-age-18 family members at 17 and 19 are registered as well. It is never too early to start talking with your neighbors about the upcoming elections. Although you may be a little nervous at first, you really don't need a script, just start by explaining who you are and why you are there: "I live over on Maple Street and I'm working to get more people involved in our political system...., or, my son lives down the block and were talking about how impersonal our political system has become." Or" I live in (a nearby town) and I'm concerned about what the Republicans are doing about (whatever)." Of course it is better when an organization is in place, better yet when it has access to VoteBuilder or similar lists so that you can approach a household knowing how frequently its residents vote, whether they are animal rights activists or members of the NRA, and so on. And with a club or campaign organization, canvassing can be targeted to districts with the highest vote potential.

Local clubs are often short-lived, and there is no magic formula for keeping them in business. The mechanisms for keeping what local groups there are in touch with each other across and entire congressional district or a state are even more fragile. The highly targeted, inexpensive, and effective network of volunteers created by Barak Obama in 2008 and expanded in 2012 showed how this can be done.[18] But this network too tended to be short-lived and proved impossible for Hillary Clinton to revive or recreate. There is nothing new about this. Every campaign must to some extent invent itself, particularly at the national or statewide level. What can best facilitate this process is the availability of a pre-existing network of local organizations ready, willing and able to connect candidates and voters. It is only through such volunteer organizations, networks, e-mail groups and regular party organizations that the groundwork of one campaign can serve as the foundation for the next. Local organizations can and will be divided as 2020 approaches on who should be the party's candidate for president, but it is important for Democrats to be democrats and to understand that we can disagree without being disagreeable, and that there are larger battles that need to fought. What best facilitates working together is, well, working together. What we can do and learn from each other in 2018 will play a major role in our ability to do anything of significance in 2020.

Endnotes

1   Http://www.rollcall.com/news/gonzales/ratings-changes-in-15-house-races. Accessed September 8, 2017.

2   John E. Leighly and Jonathan Nagler, "Turnout, Competitiveness and Candidate Policy Choices in Off-Year Elections," paper presented at the 2017 meeting of the American Political Science Association in San Francisco, CA, August 31-September 3, 2017.

3   Christopher Hare and Keith T. Poole, "The Polarization of Contemporary American Politics," 46 *Polity* (July 2014), 411-429.

4   Rachel Blum, Justin Alan Koch and Alexander R. Podkul, "Team Players: Party Loyalty and Campaign Donations," paper presented at the 2017 meeting of the American Political Science Association in San Francisco, CA, August 31-September 3, 2017.

5   William Riordan, *Plunkitt of Tammany Hall* (New York: Dutton, 1963), 51.

6   Danielle Tcholakian, "Challenging the Party Establishment," *The New York Times,* September 3, 2017, WE7.

7   Daniel Kreiss, *Taking Our Country Back: The Crafting of Networked Politics From Howard Dean to Barack Obama* (New York: Oxford University Press, 2012), 16.

8   Daniel Kreiss, *Prototype Politics: Technology-Intensive Campaigning and the Data of Democracy* (New York: Oxford University Press, 2016). 212-13.

9   Ibid. 215.

10 Ibid.

11 Richard F. Fenno, Jr., *Home Style: House Members in Their Districts* (Boston: Little, Brown and Company, 1978), 236.

12 Ibid. 237.

13 Donald P. Green and Alan S. Gerber, *Get Out the Vote: How to Increase Voter Turnout* (Washington: Brookings Institution Press, 2015), 33.

14 Ibid.

15 Robert Michels, *Political Parties: A Sociological Study of the Oligarchical Tendencies of Modern Democracy* (Glenco, IL: The Free Press, 1966, originally published in 1915).

16 David S. Broder, *The Party's Over: The Failure of Politics in America* (New York: Harper and Row, 1971).

17 Alex Fouirnaies and Andrew B. Hall, How Divisive Primaries Hurt Parties: Evidence from Near-Runoffs (May 4, 2016). Available at SSRN: https://ssrn.com/abstract=2775324.

18 Abbey Levenshus, "Online Relationship Management in a Presidential Campaign: A Case Study of the Obama Campaign's Management of Its Internet-Integrated Grassroots Effort," 22 *Journal of Public Relations Research* (Fall 2010), 313-35 provides an insightful analysis of how this network was formed.

Chapter 3

Campaign Strategies and Tactics

Executive Summary and Action Agenda

Taking back the process of finding candidates who can win in November should be one of the first priorities of citizen activists. As a first step this necessitates developing organizations that transcend the official town and county lines that define party organizations. Realistically, at most a quarter of all legislative seats in Congress and at the state level are competitive. The first priority is to target seats that have been closely contested in past. The shifting of party dynamics moving through 2018 into 2020 that might begin to tip the balance enough to attract stronger challengers and impact the calculus of redistricting in 2021 suggest that few districts are beyond redemption; but the key to victory is through what are generally classified as marginal districts.

In the last off-year general election (2014) an average of about 210,000 citizens voted in each congressional district. In districts where there were competitive primaries in both major parties voter turnout was never more than 80,000. Here is where local party activists and other volunteers– if they can coordinate with each other– can have a highly disproportionate impact on the system. Their work should begin long before the actual primary, seeking first to find a candidate who can win in November and second to prevent the kind of divisive primary that might make victory more difficult.

It is important to recognize at the outset that a balanced ticket is probably a good thing, and that unions, ethnic organizations and other organized groups cannot be dismissed out of hand because they are not with you on every issue. Once organized, the first job of any grassroots campaign is to help and persuade some of the one third of those eligible to vote that they should register. With mail-in registration in all fifty states, there are still many potential voters who find the process difficult. This is low-hanging fruit, and there is nothing more effective that volunteers can do toward winning elections than registering new voters.

Once the candidate has won the nomination or a clear path to it, he or she will have access to the increasingly sophisticated data bases of the state and national parties, but nothing is better than door-to-door work in compiling lists of real as opposed to virtual voters. There must be enough local input to be sure that the campaign message is crafted in terms of local concerns and the nature of the opposition. Next in effectiveness to a registration drive is getting out the vote on the basis of individual contacts with voters. A good canvas that identifies supporters, converts a few who are wavering, supplies absentee ballot applications, helps with early voting, and reminds supporters to vote on election day generally adds at least ten to fifteen votes per precinct. Direct mobilization has been shown to have a greater effect than candidate spending. Putting people back in politics works.

Election Day work, marking off voters at the polling place and calling those who haven't voted is absolutely essential. Combined with a registration drive, a thorough canvass and effective get-out-the-vote campaign can swing the vote by as much as ten to fifteen percent.

Action Points:

- Organization is essential, either work with the existing party structure, take it over, or organize a parallel system of clubs.
- For most offices in most parts of the country, primary elections, those in which the parties nominate their candidates, are more important and easier to influence than the November general elections.
- The single most important criteria in backing primary candidates is whether they can win in November. The best indicators are that they have strong local ties, the ability to raise money, and have won other offices.
- Registering new voters and getting supporters to the polls is far more effective and efficient than converting opponents.

- A registration drive is the first step in mapping the district, identifying supporters and recruiting other volunteers.
- Good politics is a function of good lists. The best lists come from neighbors working their neighborhoods.
- Having identified your supporters, it takes a good Election Day operation to get their actual votes.

1. What Works and What Doesn't

Issues, candidates and ideologies aside, most campaigns look pretty much alike. You don't see yard signs in the downtown areas of large cities or window signs in the country, yet you could walk into the headquarters of any campaign in the country– north, south, east, west; Republican, Democrat; incumbent or challenger– and see the same basic activities. And surprisingly little has changed over time. E-mail has made the old job of "lick 'em and stick 'em" less formidable with laptops replacing piles of brochures on every improvised desk. Torchlight parades are rare. Most states now outlaw the free beer nights that breweries would throw for their favored candidates. There are no smoke-filled rooms. But the people in those now airier rooms are doing pretty much what they did fifty years ago. Some are designing and distributing leaflets, organizing walk lists and mobilizing volunteers or paid workers; media people are preparing press releases and daily blasts as they simultaneously monitor the coverage they are getting. The candidate– if he or she is in the headquarters– is almost certainly on the phone raising money. There are volunteers compiling and refining lists of voters. Someone is working on signs. An in-house pollster or hired company is coordinating with the campaign manager. A volunteer or hired hand is doing opposition research and tracking its campaign. Early in the campaign there are people working on voter registration. At least one person is scheduling the candidate's appearances, finding surrogates where needed, and coordinating with other candidates and office holders. The list goes on.

Despite growing professionalization, what is perhaps most fascinating about these activities is how little their cost-effectiveness or general efficacy has been really studied. The day after the election, as the loser's supporters gather to collect their effects and say their goodbyes, they seldom ask whether having the paper coffee cups emblazoned with the candidates' name won any votes, or whether the get-out-the-vote flyers they hung on every door actually helped.

> The paper trail that might illuminate what actually happened– the binders filled with polling data, the hard drives filled with data bases accounting for every direct contact made with a voter– usually end up in the nearest Dumpster. Often no one even convenes a postmortem among the staff operatives, consultants and candidate to talk about what went wrong and why.[1]

There are good reasons that campaigns seldom seriously examine questions of what works and what does not. Any decent test of various techniques requires measuring its use with one sample of the population against a control group that was not exposed to the technique. But the very idea of a control group, or as the campaign manager would put it, a group whose votes we don't go after, is anathema to a serious candidate. Thus, "While much has been written on how parties raise money, relatively little has been offered on how that money is spent."[2] There are, at the same time, enough historical campaigns in similar areas with different campaign priorities, that a rough outline of what works best under what conditions is emerging. Let's look at the evidence through the major stages of a campaign.

2. Candidates

There are a handful of candidates who are more coroneted than elected. In the days of machine politics, it was possible for a total unknown party loyalist to use the organization's control of the process to win local or state office and perhaps a seat in congress. Complete unknowns can still win local offices simply because no one else wants to run. By-and-large, however, people have to know who you are. In most states today party organizations can influence but almost never control nominations, which means that celebrities, those who already hold elective office and people with enough money to buy media time are particularly advantaged whether or not they make the best candidates. And here is where citizen activists can play the absolutely vital roles of recruiting, sorting, endorsing the candidates who have both political integrity and the best chances of winning. In the wake of the still-contentious national Democratic contest between Clinton and Sanders, there will almost certainly be numerous primary fights among Democrats in 2018. As we argued in chapter 2 divisive primaries do not necessarily hurt candidates in the general election unless they are highly polarized, but they do waste resources and can leave scars that carry over into the general election. Bernie Sanders, unfortunately, gets along better with Hillary Clinton than many of his supporters get along with hers

The first and foremost priority of the old machines was to control the nominating process. The old progression of candidacy from party to local office, perhaps a foray into state politics, then Congress, as we have noted has been displaced by the lateral entry of, individuals who jump this progression by virtue of fame in another area or, more commonly, by having a lot of money. Also more common is the recruitment of candidates by ideologically motivated outside groups financing primary campaigns as a way to warn incumbents that they will face similar challenges. In many races, however, the problem is less one of candidates jumping into the fray than of finding a qualified person to give up his chosen occupation, disrupt her personal life, open himself to public criticism and scorn, and face the possibility of humiliating defeat. Realistically, candidate recruitment begins with the proposition– in a country where fewer than half of its citizens engage in so minimal a political act as voting– that few qualified candidates will be found.

In Chicago's Daley organization, as in all the old machines, candidate recruitment was part of an overall process of constructing a slate. Assembling a ticket involved "taking into consideration the interests of the various groups which make up the local Democratic Party."[3] While loyalty to the organization was important, the primary consideration was to pick candidates who could win. It was, as Milton Rakove describes it, "an exercise in science and art– in the science of constructing a well-balanced ticket and the art of pacifying the various groups that make up the electorate."[4] The decline of party machines and the controlling influence of primary elections has made it all but impossible to cover all the bases, but the principle of picking candidates primarily on their basis of their ability to win in November is still paramount. Add up all the pros and cons, in these partisan days, and the chances are that the worst Democrat running in you district will be better on 95 out of hundred issues than his or her November opponent.

Successful recruitment efforts are founded in previous organizational work. In persuading someone to run, the old machines could promise the support of a tested campaign organization, substantial financial support and immediate access to an experienced roster of campaign professionals. The greater the extent to which a popular movement can assemble such resources, the more likely it is to find capable, electable candidates. A little more than ten years ago, a group of people in my upstate New York congressional district, working largely over the internet, put together a "true blue" network of Democrats working to end Republican domination of the district. With no particular candidate in mind, they established a network of like-minded voters spanning a half dozen counties, created a roster of volunteers and secured financial pledges. By the time Kirsten Gillibrand decided to run, much of the preliminary work of organizing a campaign had been done. Redistricting, after the 2010 census, split the district and the organization more or less faded away, but there are signs of revival that are very important to both immediate and long term success. Ideally, organizing for political influence is a process not an event.

Surveys have shown that voters have rather consistently sought certain personal characteristics they look for in candidates. The most important is experience, closely followed in most surveys by honesty, intelligence and education.[5] In my own fifty years spending time on Capitol Hill, it is striking how much slimmer and better kept members of Congress have become, enough to suggest that the media have made looks an issue. Fewer and fewer members of Congress are veterans of the military, but it still appears to be of positive value, as it is to be neither "too young" nor "too old." Some prejudices are still found (and probably under-reported) particularly against women and certain ethnic groups and religions. These predilections and prejudices are eroding and can be overcome in most districts if confronted head on. "Put a lantern on it," as John F. Kennedy did in raising the question of his Roman Catholic faith at the outset of his 1960 campaign for President, preempting those who could give it a less favorable spin. In many cases, moreover, being a member of a minority can politically overcome prejudice through the pride of fellow group members. Just as there were voters who opposed Obama on racial grounds, their votes seem to have been offset by record turnout in African-American communities.

As important as these attributes might be, certain more

controllable factors count for more. The first, most and increasingly most important of these is having lots of money and/or access to it. For the first time in history, a majority of those elected to the House in 2016 were millionaires. Rich people are doubly advantaged: they both have money of their own and they know lots other people who do. Thanks to the Supreme Court, it is not just rich people we are talking about, but *very rich* people. In its 2010 ruling in the cased of *Citizens United v. Federal Elections Commission* the Court held that limits on the amounts that groups independent of actual campaign committees could make unlimited donations to independent political groups. Less publicized, but equally significant was a 2014 decision in *McCutcheon v. FEC* in which the Court ruled that ceilings on the aggregate amounts that individuals could give to political action committees, parties and so on were also unconstitutional. By elevating the phrase "money talks" from irony to constitutional doctrine, the Court dramatically changed the political landscape. The best-financed campaigns do not always win, frequently they just find ways to waste more money. Campaign consultants will tell you, on the other hand, that money can buy campaign workers but volunteers do not pay for media time or utility bills. True enough, but what they can do is to raise enough money to be viable, to use free media, to provide rent-free spaces for events, and to reach voters more effectively through neighbor-to-neighbor appeals.

For candidates, local ties are important. While national celebrities like Robert Kennedy, Hillary Clinton (and perhaps Mitt Romney) can parachute into a state and win, it is difficult– absent strong family ties– for outsiders to attract either the volunteer base or the marginal voters needed to win. Although only about half the members of the current Senate were born in the states they now represent, only a handful lack significant local roots. And that the percentage is even higher for the House. A successful candidate should have some base of community support. Even in the ethnic-charged atmosphere of Daley's Chicago, to use Rakove's example, "A Pole who has been active in the Polish National Alliance. . . would have much more attraction to slatemakers than would a Polish lawyer who has had no interest in or concern with Polish affairs."[6] Much more difficult to evaluate are questions of personality and morals. Divorce no longer seems to be a major factor, but accusations of sexual harassment seemingly are.

What may be most disturbing is the erosion in importance of the old-fashioned values of honesty and integrity. The Trumpian world of alternative truths, and his blatant violation of long accepted norms of openness, may have changed the political landscape for years to come. While I doubt that the values of corruption, collusion and nepotism have become anything like a new norm, it may no longer be important for candidates to reveal their personal financial holdings, give up financial holdings that conflict with their political roles, or separate family businesses from their political lives. Trump very cleverly hung a lantern on his conflicts of interest by blatantly making a virtue of his ability and resolve (later rescinded) to fund his own campaign. The notion that all politicians are corrupt has led many people, as Naomi Klein puts it, "to treat electoral politics as macabre entertainment. Once politics has reached such a debased state, why bother protecting it from a boor like Trump? It's a cesspool anyway, so let the game begin."[7]

Paradoxically, however, Trump's campaign itself may have shown that some old values still have legs. Citing her more than $20 million in speaking fees, the Clinton Foundation, and super-priced campaign fund-raising events, Trump's "crooked Hillary" theme eclipsed his own conflicts of interest in the 2016 polls. Clinton has never faced any legal challenges, but she, and other politicians, have had their images degraded by their fund-raising activities and connections with the rich and famous. Whether this is a cautionary tale for aspiring politicians is not clear, it may be more about spin than reality; what is clear is that the essential paradigm is changing.

There is by no means a large reservoir people dying to give up their day jobs to go into politics. I once had a student who was dating a woman whose father had agreed to run a token campaign in a district that had almost never voted for a Democrat. Having started a successful business, he thought it would be a good way to get to know his neighbors and help other Democrats running for local office. My student was with the family watching the returns come in as a Democratic landslide unfolded, and when it was announced that the businessman had won he literally burst into tears: "I don't want to be in Congress. I hate Washington," he cried, "What the hell am I going to do?" (P. S. He wound up serving four terms.) If winning is upsetting to some, losing is not fun either. Especially in seats not rated competitive, it can be difficult to find a warm body for even a token campaign. Possible candidates can sometimes be found among newer lawyers, accountants and real estate agents who can use their campaign exposure and connections as a sort of legitimate advertising. Academics have the summer and can often juggle their September and October schedules to mount credible campaigns, as can retirees. What is crucial in persuading such people is the existence of a group of volunteers ready and willing to work and enough pledges and promises of funding to mount at least a minimal campaign.

There are no rewards in politics for finishing second, but it is not trivial to have someone on the ballot if only because major upsets do occur. Eric Cantor, who many thought to be in line for the speakership, lost to an unknown in a 2014 primary largely because his Washington work had led him to ignore his district, much as Democratic Majority Leader Tom Daschle lost his seat to Republican John Thune a decade before. Indictments, deaths, unexpected retirements– stuff happens. More importantly, the seeming invulnerability of some incumbents, especially in changing districts, may be grounded less in their strengths than in the weaknesses of previous challengers. Without gainsaying the difficulty of having an impact in a district "safe" for one party or the other, there is no such thing as a sure thing. One strong campaign that moves a district from 35% to 41 or 42 may attract more volunteers, more money and perhaps a stronger candidate two years later. The shifting of a district's partisan dynamic between 2018 and 2020 will also– for better or worse– be an important part of the calculus of redistricting in 2021.

3. Organization

The period between when candidates announce their intentions and the state's filing deadlines occur, is when the role of citizen volunteers is at its maximum. If the party primary is the actual moment that counts, the winnowing period that precedes it gives an often decisive role to what we might call the "selectorate." The average population of a congressional district is roughly 740,000, roughly 300,000 of whom voted in 2016. In the last off-year election (2014) it was 210,000.[8] In districts where there were competitive primaries the turnout for either party was never more than 80,000 and was often as little as fifteen percent of eligible voters.

> While the entire American nomination system is vulnerable to capture by factions within a political party, congressional primaries, especially for the House of Representatives, are particularly vulnerable, inexpensive, targets of opportunity for national ideological groups because they operate, in most years, in near total obscurity. With the exception of elections for local school boards, congressional primaries are among the most low turnout elections in the United States. They, therefore, provide the perfect setting for interest groups within a political party to gain and exercise influence out of proportion to their size.[9]

Here is where local party activists and other volunteers– if they can coordinate with each other– can have a disproportionate impact. Their work should begin long before the actual primary, seeking first to find a candidate who can win in November, second to prevent a divisive primary that might make victory more difficult, and only third to perform an ideological litmus test. This last point, which I've argued in previous chapters, is worth reiterating. Strong party discipline, particularly in the House, has rendered the ideologies of individual members of Congress increasingly irrelevant. Even the handful of successful third party candidates– Bernie Sanders among them– join a major party caucus and follow their lead on most votes: they must if they want to get anything done. But more importantly, congressional parties have become so polarized in recent years the most conservative Democrat is more liberal than the most liberal Republican. If you want to move the Congress to the left, you must choose Democratic candidates less on the basis of their ideological purity than on their ability to win.

The more candidates there are in race, the more intense the need for vetting and working with the party structure and key groups in the district. Looking back from November, there is hardly a candidate who would not agree that their campaign began too late. When the party's selectorate is unified, the primary election becomes the first round of working the district for November. This may not be easy but it remains important. And, of course, when the prospects of victory appear slim, few viable candidates will emerge absent a strong organizational base. It is never too early to begin both fund-raising and friend-raising, if only to make it easier for strong candidates to run. There are also more subtle reasons for developing strong local organizations. Only when the folks back home are a representative's primary support group can he or she have the independence to act as an ideological free agent in the Congress. Conversely, absent a strong local base, the more a candidate must turn to the national party organizations, wealthy political action committees and others who will gladly pay the pipers who later play their tunes.

The primary building blocks of viable organizations are such legally defined areas as towns and villages, counties, city council districts, assembly districts and so on. As argued in Chapter 2, most congressional districts overlap many such jurisdictions. Once the party's nominee is chosen, it is one of his or her major challenges to bring all these diverse constituencies together. In ten states, there are fewer than ninety days between the primary and general elections in which this can be done. The more local groups have already begun this process, the more effective the campaign. Unlike the districts for most state legislators, city councils, and municipalities which often have legally mandated party organizations, congressional district organizations must be voluntarily created. Whether this is done by official party leaders from a variety of the legally-mandated districts, by informal citizen groups, or a combination of both, it is an important step toward victory.

A major organizational problem with any campaign is that of defining its relations with other organizations. The members and supporters of various progressive single-interest groups may be only peripherally interested in the campaign or even see it is a rival for funding and membership. It is a major task of any successful campaign, as Michael Waltzer once put it, "to get people into the same bed who never imagined they could take a peaceful walk together."[10] Gaining the support of an interest group begins with the recognition on the part of the campaign that you are not going to win their support by pointing to your stands on other issues, and, on the part of the group, that while you might not give them all that they want, the alternative is worse. It behooves any successful campaign to reach out to sympathetic groups from the outset, to bring their leaders in, if possible, under the campaign tent. Absolute candor is vital here— you are dealing with people who know their stuff– and if your differences are real but marginal they may want to keep their support quiet; but ties with special interests are not only avenues to voters but access to information: who can better tell about problems with military hospitals than members of veterans groups? Some advocates of high tech campaigns argue that intermediary groups have lost their importance as candidates develop their own issue-segmented data bases. This both ignores the fact that these groups themselves can provide significant inputs to those algorithms but provide direct contacts to trusted voters themselves.

These contacts can also be useful in other ways. A group like lawyers, gays, or professors for Jones might bring people out who would not come to a less-specialized fund-raiser. Special groups such as these also provide a way of dispersing titles among supporters.

The most important, and sometimes most difficult of these problems are in dealing with other campaigns. Off-year congressional candidates do not have to worry about a Clinton or a Trump, but they do have to worry about senators and sheriffs, local officials and party regulars. Even so simple an issue as whether to have single candidate yard signs or those promoting the entire slate can be surprisingly troublesome. There just aren't any good rules, as you work in a campaign or try to build an organization, in which the existing party leaders and your campaign don't see eye to eye, or where your pro-choice candidate for Congress is on the same ticket as an anti-abortion State Senator. All things considered, a balanced ticket is probably an asset if only because each of its component candidates can increase turnout for the entire ticket. If you are running a campaign filled with volunteers and a newly active club, working with the regular party organization can pose problems. Precinct captains who have held their "jobs" for years may resent volunteers intruding on their turf, even if they have not worked the district for years. They may have cohorts of relatives and friends who turn out in sufficient numbers to keep them winning, but that doesn't mean they are still working. At the height of the club movement's power in the fifties and sixties, James Q. Wilson very perceptively described the tensions that often arose between amateur Democrats oriented toward particular candidates and issues, and the regular organization types whose interests were more toward organizational maintenance.[11]

4. Voter Registration

Of citizens 18 years and older, some 30% are not registered to vote. Discounting felons and those ineligible to vote for other legal reasons– such as severe mental illness or failure to establish residence– more than one person in four chooses not to become eligible to vote.[12] Although the turnout of non-Hispanic African Americans is generally three to five percent lower than that of non-Hispanic Caucasians, race is much less a major factor in voluntary non-registration than it was fifty years ago, though this may be changing as growing number of states have recently passed voter identification laws that appear to have clear discriminatory effects. Poverty and low education rates are generally the demographic variables most closely linked to low registration rates, as is ethnicity with 44% of self-identified Asian citizens and 43% of Hispanics not registered.[13] Registration and voting also increases with age: less than 25% of 18-34 year olds voted in 2014 as compared with nearly 60 per cent of citizens over 65.

Part of the problem is that in many states registering to vote is a more complicated process than that of actually casting a ballot. And there is growing evidence that persons with disabilities, visual problems in particular, face particular barriers in all but a handful of states.[14] Among the tens of millions of unregistered voters are some who refuse on principle– Don't Vote, It Only Encourages the Bastards– as a popular bumper sticker reads. For most, as the economist Anthony Downs once wrote, "every rational man decides to vote just as he makes all other decisions: if the returns outweigh the costs, he votes, if not, he abstains."[15] For candidates and their supporters, any effort that helps to decrease the perceived "costs" of registration, or increase the benefits is to mine an enormous, generally untapped mother lode of potential votes. In the 2016 presidential election, more than thirty million more citizens stayed home rather than vote for either Trump or Clinton. Today, more than ever, "it is easier to bring a new voter into the system than it is to induce an old partisan to change sides."[16]

How can this be done? Most importantly and obviously, we can lower the costs of voting by bringing the opportunity directly to the unregistered. Under the Motor Voter law all fifty states must allow mail-in registration. Ten states also allow full registration by e-mail, while another three offer limited access on line. Even then, the task can be confusing, and costly in terms of time. With volunteer help at the door, these costs can be virtually erased. Carrying application forms or mobile wi-fi units, volunteers can guide citizens through the registration process in a matter of minutes. To the extent that citizens actually perform some sort of cost-benefit analysis in deciding whether to vote, we emphasize the cost side because the perceived benefit side of the equation is much more difficult to control. A primary determinant of voter turnout, as one recent study puts it, is "the level of uncertainty in the national campaign contest."[17] The more uncertain the outcome, in other words, or the greater the perceived differences between the candidates, the more people will see it in their interest to vote. Many state election calendars, unfortunately, require potential voters to register before most campaigns heat up. Registration drives in these areas must be forward looking, or sign people up after a divisive national election or in the immediate wake of a controversial national event or controversy.

The point is to register Democrats. As small "d" democrats, it would be unseemly to turn down other citizens; but the point of a partisan registration drive is to target areas and individuals with a high potential of being Democrats.

Once again it's a matter of picking cherries where the cherries are. We will discuss targeting anon, but the point here is that there is nothing that volunteers can do that is more effective toward winning elections than registering new voters. And it can be done any time– years, and months ahead, and, in some states, right up until Election Day.

Would it be that the issue were that simple. For many nonvoters the "costs" of voting go beyond time and confusion. There are voters, and this is a very tricky issue to poll, whose general suspicion of anything to do with the government leads them to believe that registering to vote will subject them to new taxes or other penalties. One survey found that twenty per cent of adults who had never voted expected their ballot to be marked for later examination, another twelve percent thought they would have to declare out loud who they were voting for.[18] Many others see little connection between voting and public policy. At the same time, a recent study by the Pew Research Center shows "that the unregistered population is not entirely unengaged from civic life." Indeed, the study found that, "more than 40 percent of the unregistered cared who would win the presidency in 2016, and some indicated that they could be motivated to register in the future, though many also feel that the voting process does not affect the way governing decisions are made. These findings suggest that opportunities exist to engage segments of the unregistered population."[19] As Murphy and I wrote in 1974:

> The key to voter registration is often social pressure. People vote because they are embarrassed not to, because their

neighbors do, because it is accepted as one of the duties of a loyal American, or simply because someone asks them to. One reason that upper- and middle-income citizens are more likely to vote than the poor is that social pressures encouraging voting are much stronger in more affluent communities.[20]

Partly because voter registration has long been treated as a non-partisan civic exercise, most registration drives have been conducted by non-profits not parties. The parties' increasingly sophisticated ability to micro-target demographic groups, however, provides a growing ability to target and register only those most likely to support particular candidates. A "birthday program," for example, targeting African Americans when they turned eighteen, added thousands of Obama voters to the rolls in 2012. Once particular area have been targeted, direct mail appeals can have some effect, but the social pressure implicit in personal visits, with its combined power to explain the secret ballot and the process of registration is far more effective. After volunteers selectively canvas their own neighborhoods, the first step is to prioritize areas of Democratic strength, sending volunteers to them, and using phone and mail appeals to those further down on the list. In areas of high home ownership, voter files can be compared with property tax reports to show which households do not have registered voters. Sometimes electric company lists and city directories can be used to locate potential voters. The better one knows the neighborhood, the more common sense kicks in: if there are two registered voter in a house and three cars there is a good chance of finding an unregistered teenager. A fading bumper sticker for Trump is not a good sign.

It is best, particularly in neighborhoods not known to the volunteer, to have volunteers travel in pairs, preferably male and female, and to deploy at least one bi-lingual person in districts with known ethnic minorities. Most importantly, each campaign should provide a briefing sheet that explains local election laws in some detail, and a handout to remind residents of important dates and a phone number or e-mail address to contact if they have any problems. Before sending volunteers into a neighborhood, the campaign should first contact the local party organization and groups like labor unions that may already have targeted the same neighborhoods. Scripts can be found in any one of a dozen campaign manuals, and many volunteers will ask for one; but a neighborly conversational approach probably works best. Typically, a registration drive marks the beginning of a formal campaign, and it should be seen as an entry level platform for an increasingly refined process of voter identification. Its purpose is not simply to put new voters on the rolls but to serve as the first cut in the process of mapping the district and of getting voters to think about the upcoming election. And it is also an opportunity to find new recruits.

It is never too early to recruit volunteers—others to go door-to-door—and for those uncomfortable doing that, to answer the phones, prepare mailings, and so on. I've never known of a campaign that had too many volunteers, yet it is surprising how many recruitment opportunities are lost. Every time the candidate meets a potential volunteer, or someone offers to help there should be an immediate follow-up. Some campaigns go so far as to always have a supply of mailing lists and envelopes on hand just to keep people involved.

Perhaps the most fruitful orchards for picking cherries are those particularly targeted by an increasingly anti-immigrant Republican Party. Hispanics are, of course, the largest such group, but in the past ten years, in the borough of Queens, New York with carefully crafted Chinese and Korean language phone drives, the largely Korean non-profit, MinKwon, registered nearly sixty thousand voters, nearly doubling the percentage of Asians voters in the district and electing its first member of the state assembly.[21] Minority under enrollment is the soft underbelly of Republican hegemony.

5. Raising Money

Early in the campaign it is absolutely vital for the candidate and his or her supporters to get around the district and meet with potential supporters. These meet-and-greet sessions are essentially friend-raisers rather than fund-raisers, though the boundaries between the two are not clear. What professional fund-raisers will tell you is that you must go first for the big money with one-on- one contacts. To have a $100 a person event with friends and neighbors who could easily afford to give $2000 lets them off the hook. It is discouraging but true that money counts: in 2012 better than 93 percent of the biggest spenders in House races won and 79 percent in Senate races.[22] Thus one of the first priorities in every campaign is for the candidate to get on the phone and go after the big bucks. The acronym EMILYs List, an organization that supports pro-choice women, stands for "Early Money Is Like Yeast– it makes the dough rise." It is often important in getting the help of organizations and politicians that use a candidate's ability to raise money as a sign of viability. It is also vital in planning media aspects of a campaign lest the desirable time slots be taken. Catherine Shaw describes a candidate who put off his media buys until October only to find that "basically Saturday cartoons were left."[23] Incumbents have an obvious advantage in accessing early gifts, so do millionaires who can fund their own campaigns. It would be nice to be able to say, as an unsuccessful candidate for mayor of Washington, D. C. once did, that "It's not how much money you raise. It's how you spend your money."[24] In academic terms, most studies show that "there are strongly diminishing marginal returns to campaign spending."[25] But although prudence and care are recommended, under-financed campaigns are almost invariably losing campaigns. Some threshold amount– enough to pay salaries, pay for phone and internet lines, open at least one office, and pay for some form of media– is essentially an entry fee to serious candidacy.

After roughly forty years of almost unchallenged incumbency, Democrats lost their majority in the House of Representatives in 1994. Writing in the wake of that election, Eismer and Pollock presciently observed that,

> Democratic survivors will probably be able
> to fund adequately their 1996 campaigns.
> But it will require more hustling, an
> unappealing prospect that may urge

some into retirement. Between defending incumbents and attempting to win back seats lost in 1994, the resources of labor PACs will be stretched very thin. Even with the support of labor PACs, Democrats have lagged behind Republicans in money for challengers.[26]

Where will new Democratic money come from? It would be nice to be able to say in 2018 that thousands of pissed-off Democrats, minorities and gays will pony up, and that is the challenge of the next four years. As we move in that direction, however, Sutton's Law prevails. When asked why he always robbed banks, Willie (the Actor) Sutton's reply was "because that's where the money is." And so it is that Democrats must start with those who can most afford to contribute.

Among the straws that broke the back of Hillary Clinton's campaign was the issue of her secret, mega-bucks briefings of such Wall Street giants as Goldman-Sacks. I'd like to think that secrecy was the issue here, and that Clinton handled it badly, but both Sanders and (ironically) Trump managed to make it an issue. But let us just make it clear that not all rich people drool and move their lips as they read the Wall Street Journal. Indeed there are many citizens with substantial resources who are quite liberal, not just on social issues but economic issues as well (e.g., Warren Buffet's lament that his secretary paid income taxes at a higher rate than he does). Well folks, that's where the money is, and the first step in a viable campaign is to find it.

Getting people with money to contribute to a candidate

or cause generally involves three steps: first, finding the people who actually have money; second, making the case for them to contribute; and finally, asking. If you get ten people in a room virtually all them will enjoy helping to identify those of their friends and neighbors who have money. Seven or eight out the ten will gladly go out and make the case for the campaign. You are lucky if you can get three who are comfortable doing the actual ask. Often it is more effective to do the "ask" in person with two people– one to make the case, the other to close the deal. The most common mistake people make in asking for money is asking too little. Imagine yourself with a comfortable income, being approached, hearing the pitch, and being asked for five dollars. It's an insult. Ask for five thousand and it's easy for someone to give you a thousand, but no one will give you five thousand if you ask for one.

In a district with hundreds of thousands of voters, it is all but impossible for the candidate personally to put the arm on more than a relatively small number of potential voters. Events– from large dinners and rallies to neighborhood "meet and greets"– have the added advantage of giving the candidate exposure, providing the opportunity to recruit new volunteers, and sometimes getting coverage in the media. But these events must be carefully planned. Nothing is more embarrassing than an audience of twenty in a hall that holds two hundred. I personally like the old-fashioned, home-based coffee or cocktail party. An advance person makes a brief pitch, the candidate arrives with an aide, speaks and answers questions for fifteen minutes and is hustled to the next home; the advance person gets feed-back, makes a pitch for money and volunteers and says good night.

A reasonably fit candidate can do twenty or thirty of these events a day. Small events such as these, and direct asks for money have the advantage of being virtually cost free.

Direct mail and telemarketing campaigns, like registration drives are cost effective in direct relationship to the planning that goes into them, both in targeting potential donors and crafting targeted messages. And they must be carefully targeted to be cost/effective. The internet is much cheaper and many campaigns now prefer it to other media. Hillary Clinton raised roughly a third of her 2016 campaign funds through e-mails. But aside from face-to face appeals, it matters less how potential donors are contacted than whether they were contacted at all. Just as an earlier generation of media targets learned how to ignore political snail mail, and their children found ways to block phone calls, we are reaching a point where the on line trash baskets of voters are beginning to overflow.

If you are lucky, a campaign's pool of volunteers may include a professional fund-raiser and a lawyer or two. If not, it might be wise either to outsource some of the work, or at the least bring in a consultant to work with a local fund-raising team. Targeting, in terms of both audience and media, is an increasingly technical art especially when it comes to fundraising. Having the endorsements of the local party, and various groups like Emily's list or the National Committee for an Effective Congress can give a campaign access to a lot of professional help with these issues. And of course there are the National and State Party Committees.

The notion that all politics is local is increasingly challenged by our broken system of campaign finance which has both nationalized political money and vastly enhanced the influence of a handful of enormously wealthy families. The three keys to at least partially countering these forces are those of expanding the base of small donors, using resources better, and mobilizing volunteers. The easiest way to channel small donations is through the national, state, House and Senate campaign committees of the Democratic Party; but giving at the local level, where campaigns are, we hope, run in terms of district priorities is far more effective, and it has public relations value as well. For those not living in or near competitive campaigns, you can start with the appendices to this book to locate campaigns in your area where you contributions can have an impact. Volunteering your time is even better.

6. Hunting Butterflies

In the 1790s, Thomas Jefferson and James Madison traveled through the northeast allegedly collecting butterflies. What they were actually collecting were the allies and friends who became the core of what is now the Democratic Party. I don't think anybody knows what kinds of lists they came north with, but you can be sure that they knew in advance who they wanted to talk with and who they did not. Good politics begins with good lists.

The national committees and the senatorial and congressional campaign committees are, as we noted in chapter 2, increasingly involved in compiling, refining and sharing data bases. Nothing is more central to a successful campaign. Computers have revolutionized political lists, allowing a super-segmentation of voter lists and an ever-increasing ability to micro-target fund-raising, media and get-out the vote efforts. In its essence, however, it remains both a traditional science and art of trying to determine in advance what voters are most and least likely to vote for your candidate. What Issenberg calls the "hard ID" voters, those who have explicitly told a canvasser or caller for whom they will vote, are still the gold standard of all campaigns. "But no campaign," as he points out, "has ever been able to hard-ID every voter in the universe, or even a majority of them."[27] Not only are the costs prohibitive, but even self-reported voting intentions are not completely reliable. Out of a desire to be friendly, or out of simple perversity, people lie. They also change their minds. In fact, since the early voting behavior studies of the 1960s, many political scientists have actually been able to predict how people will vote with greater accuracy than have the voters themselves. In the 2016 elections, models based on demographic factors and past election returns often turned out to be more likely accurately to predict Donald Trump's victory than the polls that asked people who they intended to support.

As noted in chapter 2, what modern campaign consultants have been able to do is to accumulate multiple years of polls and canvas results and write "statistical algorithms based on known information about a small set of voters," and use these to "extrapolate to find other voters who looked– and presumably thought and acted– like them, and then treating "these virtual IDs as an effective replacement for hard IDs where it couldn't get them.[28] Beyond poll results, the computer models can suck up reams of individualized data from motor vehicle ownership to military service. It can tell you who subscribes to what magazines and newspapers, gives to some charities, and (in some states) are registered to carry firearms. It can include lists of everyone who has given more than $100 to a national political campaign. Not all suburban, Italian-American drivers of Dodge Ram trucks who shop at Walmart and play fantasy football vote the same way, and that may not be a usable category; but the more narrowly focused each statistical type becomes through testing and retesting, the closer each virtual ID can be used to replace a hard one. And even fairly simple algorithms can be enormously useful as, for example, by soliciting money only from those who are registered Democrats who have given previously, you can save a ton of money in postage.

It is difficult not to feel some discomfort with the idea of "managing" voters by targeting communications and ignoring the masses. It too easily conjures images of creating managed citizens.[29] Given that the other side is also becoming more adept at mobilizing their supporters, micro targeting can only exacerbate polarization. In many ways, however, these fears are overblown. Writing about the Obama campaign's use of these algorithms Kreiss argues that critics "generally overstate the control that campaign staffers and political consultants have over the electorate." In its use of computational management of an increasingly sophisticated data base, its

> Control of supporters' actions was always probabilistic not deterministic. Control was limited to increasing the likelihood that people would take particular actions for the campaign. It was confined to easily measured domains, such as sign-ups to

the e-mail list and donations. While the campaign used data to coordinate its volunteers and new media applications . . . there was plenty of volunteer agency in the interstices of these systems.[30]

The role of volunteers is absolutely crucial in filling these gaps between computer models and real, as opposed to virtual citizens.

The most important role of local volunteers is to provide ongoing human feedback to the computer models. Even as American voters have become more polarized, there is still an enormous amount of slack and dynamism in the system. All the campaign manuals you might buy, for example, will tell you not to bother knocking on the doors of registered, regular voters of the opposition party. And this is generally true in the weeks before the election when your presence might actually awaken them to vote. But putting people back in politics means reinstating the old machine politician's knack for both mobilizing voters and using volunteers to listen to what rank-and-file voters are saying. And while political polarization is a fact of life, a very large slice of the electorate remains uncommited with their partisan identities relatively fluid. The "big surprise" of the 2016 presidential election was, supposedly, how many white, working class, usually-Democratic voters went for Trump. Of equal, though less noticed, was the switch of suburban women to the Democrats, and the long-range move of Hispanics toward the Party. Dr. Murphy's follow-up study of the effects of the anti-war student involvement in campaigns, found "preference increases" of between 3.9

and 17.2% among contacted voters.[31] Voters may well be more set in their opinions than they were in the 1970s, but the point is that there is still enough slack in the system that voter preferences— especially when prodded through face-to-face contact— may be more fungible than many professional practitioners may think.

Let's get back to picking cherries. Registration lists and past voting records are the time-tested starting points, but they are by no means definitive. There are more people who refuse to identify themselves with either party than as Republicans or Democrats. Data bases can show which of these voters are inclined to vote one way or the other, but there are still large numbers who cannot be classified. Of those registered with a party, moreover, many are partisans in disguise. And with those who are registered with parties, many are there more from habit than conviction.

7. Spending Money

Here's the deal: before you spend a nickel in a campaign, you must set your priorities. This is, essentially, the job of a professional campaign manager. But just as he or she might be considered both the CEO and CFO of the campaign (not to mention the candidate) there should be some kind of executive committee to help set priorities. It has been said that half of the money spent in the typical campaign is wasted, the problem is that we don't know which half.

Generally campaigns work through four overlapping stages: enrollment, identification, persuasion and mobilization. Voters must first be registered and volunteers signed up, they must know who the candidate is and for what office, persuaded to vote for him or her, and finally reminded actually to cast a ballot. The enrollment stage, registering voters and signing up volunteers is actually continuous and cannot be started to early. Nor can it ever be too early to begin opposition research, organization, fundraising and mapping the district. All of this work essentially is conducted one-on-one and behind the scenes.

The starting point of the public campaign is to gain name recognition as the base point for establishing connections. Yard signs, bumper stickers, buttons and billboards are traditional vehicles that put names in play and hopefully link them to a more general campaign motif such as party affiliation, a slogan or just a color scheme that will run through the weeks ahead. Two studies have shown that randomly placed get-out-the-vote signs increase turnout by a percentage or two. People who display lawn signs are more likely to vote than those who don't, and there may even be some modest effects on candidate preferences. They are also expensive, particularly signs which are increasingly likely to be stolen or defaced. The very tech savvy people in Obama's campaign were skeptical enough of the efficacy of these devices that they essentially treated them more as aspects of the fund-raising efforts than advertising. In local races– particularly in those that rely heavily on volunteers– signs, enough at least to match the opposition, may be needed to keep up morale, and buttons may be useful in opening doors. Every campaign must have at least one basic brochure. Some advertising is necessary if only to give volunteers and funders a sense of seriousness. And if radio, television and print media are cost effective, money should be set aside for professional production costs. To spend a few thousand dollars producing an ad that costs hundreds of thousands to broadcast is throwing money away.

Paid media move up from name recognition to persuasion. Increasingly, campaign professionals are moving from general media to those more narrowly focused, finding the best media for reaching specific groups. To take an obvious example, you don't buy time on hip hop radio stations to pitch your position on Medicare. Then there are questions of cost-effectiveness. A candidate running for congress in southern California, for example, who buys ad time on a Los Angeles television station is either very rich or desperate as he or she is covering the costs of a message that will appear in 24 other districts. This is not the place for a detailed analysis of these questions, particularly since they will differ markedly from one type of district to another. But the under-lying rule is simple: media choices should be made not because this is the way it has always been done, but out of a shrewd calculation as to how cost-effectively they can reach your voter base. Issenberg credits Republican strategist Timmy Teepill with thinking "of politics not as an activity conducted in well-bounded geographic spaces but as one that pulsed through networks of people linked by common interests."[32] Old media people thought of cost-effectiveness in terms of "CPMs," or costs per thousands of people reached. In the new politics it is who gets reached, with what, through what media and at what cost.

One more point. With any media you are in competition not with the opposition so much as with every other commodity and cause targeting the same audience. We have all gotten good at ignoring the literally hundreds of messages beamed at us daily by people who are getting more and more clever at getting our attention. So when the candidate's carefully crafted flyer arrives in your mailbox, it probably arrives with an equally alluring ad from a real estate agent, a piece from a dentist offering to improve your smile, and a sure cure for hemorrhoids. So unless your hemorrhoids are acting up or you are in the market for a new house, all four brochures probably go into the same recycling bin. So whether your media of choice is direct mail, the internet, TV, radio (too often ignored) it must be both targeted and able to penetrate our skepticism.

The internet, particularly e-mails specifically target to individual voters, has the potential to turn many of the old rules on their heads. In particular, it can, along with advances in targeting, personalize contacts with persuadable voters, providing opportunities, virtually unavailable through traditional media, for communications that work in both directions, listening to voters at the same as you are trying to influence them, getting instant feedback on what works and what doesn't, and genuinely giving people the sense that they are involved in the campaign. Not the least, the new media provide opportunities to make large numbers of volunteers partners in the campaign. But please, avoid the temptation— because it only takes a few clicks— to overload inboxes with the electronic equivalent of junk mail.

8. Winning Votes

What most campaign consultants insist from the outset is that a campaign stay on message. "It's the economy, stupid," it said on signs posted all over Bill Clinton's campaign offices in 1994 as a reminder not to get side-tracked. Ideally, it is argued, everything the campaign does should be considered through the lens of an over-arching theme: green yard signs if the environment is the issue, blue signs and Democrat in big letters if the party match is good. Out of necessity and choice, most modern campaigns run wholesale, one major central supplier working through a spotty network of retail vote seekers, relying largely on paid media to push the product. Mobilization not conversion, getting your voters to the polls is the norm.

But although Democrats are the majority party, skewed demographics, voting rules, gerrymandering and the lower turnout rates of the party's supporters necessitate extra effort. The most sophisticated election analysts– such as Rasmussen, Sabato, Rothenberg and Abramowitz– suggest that Democrats need to increase their popular vote by at least seven per cent in order to capture a majority of the House in 2018. The twin keys to gaining such a margin are in the areas of voter registration and getting out the vote; but working with Democrats alone will probably not suffice. Going after independents– who are generally less sophisticated and less informed voters– is tricky but necessary. Even more than with party stalwarts, the efforts must be clearly targeted both in terms of voters and messages. We have seen how increasingly sophisticated surveys and computer algorithms have enabled candidates to target individual voters. They are also getting more sophisticated in telling us how to package the campaign message: what issues, especially should be emphasized with what voters. This is not to say that a candidate's stands on issues should be driven by polls, in fact if there is anything worse than being out of step with the voters it coming across as phony or slick. What it most certainly does mean is being able to craft the campaign message in terms of local concerns and circumstances. What works in California may not work in Texas, and the more that national figures attempt to define the issues of the year, the more it may behoove local candidates to assert their independence.

Here again, the heavy hand of Supreme Court's campaign finance decisions have a major impact. Under current law, major contributors, while they are still marginally constrained in helping individual candidates may make virtually unlimited, virtually anonymous contributions to independent committees. In 2012 alone, one study found, nearly one billion dollars that could not legally have been spent in 2008 was used by such outside groups to influence the election.[33] Aside from the enormous distorting influence of such money on the whole political process, a less noticed but also significant impact of these independent expenditures lies in their impact on individual campaigns which are increasingly less in control of their own messages. By law, the only limit on these groups is that their expenditures are totally uncoordinated with the campaign. Whether voters know that or not, your message may not be in your hands.

What are in your hands are the messages you send. For many voters, their contact with a volunteer may be virtually the only campaign message they attend to. The content of political messages is going to vary much according to local conditions and—especially with campaigns run largely by volunteers—in response to the feedback from constituents they provides. A few of the guidelines that might prove useful are the following: first, and most obviously, the media world has changed. Newspapers do have the advantage of communicating with opinion leaders and although they become increasingly less cost-effective as Election Day nears, their endorsements help. Television remains a powerful medium and even if at least half of the time they will be viewed on a hand-held screen or in a tavern where the sound is turned off, the power of strong visuals is enormous. Why so many candidates still produce talking head commercials, or spend thousands buying time to show poorly produced spots is beyond me. Television can also be prohibitively expensive when candidates are paying for markets that include many other districts, or when the time buys are made too late in the campaign to be effectively placed. Radio has similar cost inefficiencies, but has the advantage of playing to much more clearly segmented audiences. Campaigns often forget that all of these media are often hungry for good local content news, sending a brief clip for the evening news is like getting free advertising. With all of these media, the biggest mistake of most campaigns is to focus more on coverage than content. A really effective commercial that airs less frequently is better than a bad one endlessly repeated. It is ironic but true that most candidates will spend more time preparing a speech before sixty Rotary Club members than working on a commercial or press release that will be seen by thousands. Every candidate, moreover, should have a short, well-thought-out statement on all of the dozen or so issues likely to arise at candidate forums or in contacts with the media. Nothing is more embarrassing than a candidate hemming and hawing on the evening news.

In the long run, or crudely done, they make come back to bite, but as distasteful as they often are, most studies clearly show that negative commercials work. Perhaps the best way of going negative without feeling a little dirty, is to avoid direct attacks. Tony Schwartz's "daisy" ad for Lyndon Johnson in 1964 was shown only once, but may be the most famous political ad ever run. It showed a little girl counting the petals of a daisy. With her count morphing into a countdown, the girl's image faded into the mushroom cloud of a nuclear bomb. "The stakes are high," the screen read, "Vote for Johnson." The ad was bitterly criticized by many who said that the ad unfairly attacked Johnson's opponent as a dangerous warmonger. But as Schwartz pointed out, the ad said nothing about Barry Goldwater, what it did with the images was to resonate with ideas about Senator Goldwater that were already in peoples' heads. And that truly is one of the best ideas in all kinds of political advertising, and it underlines the importance of polling and other forms of feedback—especially that from volunteers going door-to-door— to find out what's in people's heads and how each message from the campaign can be made to resonate with it.

One final point on content. Gloom and doom ads may work in the short run, and running against Congress (while running for it) is popular even among incumbents. Aside from the systemic effects of such campaigns, the danger is that they threaten to depress turnout, even in the short run. And depressing turnout tends to hurt Democrats. If the system is as dysfunctional as many Americans already believe, what is the sense in participating in its rituals? The real issue is not one of changing the basic system but of changing the people who are causing it to fail.

9. GOTV

No matter how good the message, how efficient the campaign, the bottom line is getting out your vote on or before Election Day. The GOTV effort, coincidentally, is the campaign arena in which volunteers able to have their greatest impact. Virtually all campaign professionals agree that with good lists going door to door is the single most effective way to get out the vote. As Green and Gerber put it,

> The more personal the interaction between campaign and potential voter, the more it raises a person's chances of voting. Door-to-door canvassing by enthusiastic volunteers is the gold-standard mobilization tactic; chatty, unhurried phone calls seem to work well too. Automatically dialed, prerecorded GOTV phone calls, by contrast, are utterly impersonal and, evidently, wholly ineffective at getting people to vote.[34]

This is one area of campaign management that has been systematically studied, and virtually every field experiment comparing the use of different methods has confirmed Green and Gerber's basic finding The effects, moreover, can be quite substantial, adding as much or more than seven percent to a candidate's vote total. Compiling numerous GOTV studies, moreover, Green and Gerber were able to compare the relative cost-effectiveness of various ways of trying to affect turnout such as leafleting (which had trivial effects), robo calls (none), direct mail (trivial) targeted phone calls by trained volunteers (good), and so on.[35] This analysis is must reading for any campaign team. Effective get out the vote drives are founded in sound research, with algorithms or, preferably, the results of canvassing. They are premised on the time tested notions that mobilizing your latent supporters is much more efficient than converting others, and that attempts to convert close to Election Day may have the contrary effect of turning out the opposition.

The basic canvass identifying sure and likely supporters, is done before Election Day. Thirty-three states now allow early voting, and almost a third of the voters in those states have availed themselves of that opportunity, so it is crucial to know what the deadlines and procedures are. Most states also allow absentee ballots which also have application and submission deadlines. The opportunities these procedures open are enormous, most obviously in contained communities such as retirement homes and college dormitories. Volunteers cannot only help residents apply for ballots, but make follow-up calls to make sure that people actually vote. Knowing who has actually voted, moreover, sharply eases the GOTV work needed on Election Day.

Targeting and records of which voters have already cast their ballots in hand, what happens on Election Day is perhaps most crucial. Whether because of fight with the boss or a hot date, the chances are that some people will simply forget to vote. After all, it's just a Tuesday. For political activists and candidates that Tuesday may be Labor Day, New Years, Thanksgiving and the Fourth of July rolled into one, but for most voters it's just another Tuesday. All of your work may go for naught unless and until you close the deal on this one day. First thing in the morning, at every polling place, there should be a volunteer. Every party on the ballot (or every candidate in a primary) is entitled to sit behind or beside the official election judges ostensibly to challenge fraudulent voters, but largely, in practice, as the major component of the GOTV effort. There should be three lists of registered voters with the names of those who have already cast and early or absentee ballot crossed off and a contact number and/or e-mail address. (Some states do the work of listing those who have voted for you). As each new voter appears, his or her name is crossed off until about two hours before the polls close when a runner should be dispatched to take one of the lists to people manning a phone (or standing in a nearby public area using their cell phones). Any of your candidate's identified supporters should then be contacted and reminded to vote. An hour later, the revised second list is used to again contact those who haven't voted. That's it. Simple as it sounds this tried and trusted election-day routine generally can be counted on to add at least ten or fifteen voters to the total in each precinct.

10. The Anatomy of Victory

For all the research that has been done by political scientists, pollsters, campaign consultants and statisticians, campaigns and elections are as much art as science. We know a lot about how voters decide and about how those decisions can be influenced. But there is a lot that we don't. What we do know can be summarized in pretty simple terms. First, nothing works better than personal contact. Getting the candidate out and around is the starting point, putting real people on the ground is far and away the next best thing. Second, it is easier and generally more effective to influence who actually votes than how they vote. Of all the things an individual can do to change the face of American politics, the easiest and most effective is that of getting like-minded individuals to vote. Money is, of course, important in politics, but we know a lot less about the effects of campaign spending than we do about the impact of volunteers.

> Direct mobilization in the form of party and candidate contact significantly increases the extent to which most citizens are familiar with the candidates in congressional races and increases the extent to which citizens are able to place the candidates on an ideological scale. Further, direct mobilization appears to have a much greater effect than candidate spending. Indeed candidate spending may even have a negative effect.[35]

It is certainly easier to go on line and make a campaign contribution. It may be even more effective to talk with your neighbors. A rough estimate is that there are roughly six hundred precincts or voting districts in every congressional district. If volunteers in each of those districts can persuade just fifteen new people to register and vote, and if their GOTV work has the typical effect of turning out ten more, that's a minimum swing of twenty-five times six hundred or 15,000 votes. There are more than twenty congressional districts where that amount of extra Democratic votes would have changed the outcome in 2016. Add the expected swing away from the party controlling the White House and it should be clear that volunteers can make the difference. It should also be noted that these contacts often have cumulative effects in the sense that they often discover other potential volunteers and financial donors. There are no better ways of building an organization.

Endnotes

1 Sasha Issenberg, *The Victory Lab: The Secret Science of Winning Campaigns* (New York: Broadway Books, 2013), 68.

2 Brian J. Box, *Back in the Game: Political Party Campaigning in an Era of Reform* (Albany: State University of New York Press, 2013), 10.

3 Milton Rakove, *Don't Make No Waves. . . Don't Back No Losers: An Insider's Analysis of the Daley Machine* (Bloomington: Indiana University Press), 96.

4 Ibid., 97.

5 The only systematic study I know of is the rather dated summary in David A. Luethold, *Electioneering in a Democracy* (New York: John Wiley and Sons, 1994). More recent polls and the websites of groups like the League of Women Voters are generally consistent with his list.

6 Rakove, 97.

7 Naomi Klein, *No Is Not Enough: Resisting Trump's Shock Politics and Winning the World We Need* (Chicago: Haymarket Books, 2017), 42.

8 Much of the data provided here is taken from Thom File, *Who Votes? Elections and the American Electorate: 1978-2014* (Washington: Bureau of the Census, 2015) and available on line from https://www.census.gov/content/dam/Census/library/publications/2015/demo/p20-577.pdf

9 Elaine C. Camarck, *Increasing Turnout in Congressional Primaries* (Washington, DC: The Brookings Institution Center for Effective Public Management, 2014), 8.

10 Michael Walzer, *Political Action: A Practical Guide to Movement Politics* (Chicago: Quadrangle Books, 1971), 40.

11 James Q. Wilson, *The Amateur Democrat* (Chicago: University of Chicago Press, 1962).

12 U. S. Census Bureau, Reported Voting and Registration by Race, Hispanic Origin, Sex and Age, November 2016. https://census.gov/data/tables/time-series/demo/voting-and-registration/p20-580.html. Accessed September 10, 2017.

13 Ibid.

14 Susan Mizner and Eric Smith, *Access Denied: Barriers to Online Voter Registration for Citizens with Disabilities* (New York: American Civil Liberties Union, 2015).

15 Anthony Downs, *An Economic Theory of Democracy* (New York: Harper and Row, 1961), 123.

16 E. E Schattschneider, *The Semisovereign People: A Realist's View of Democracy in America* (New York: Holt, Rinehart and Winston, 1960), 112. Despite some rather dubious uses of statistics, this is one of the most provocative, still-relevant books in the canon of political science.

17 Lyn Ragsdale and Jerrold G. Rusk, *The American Nonvoter* (New York: Oxford University Press, 2017), 24.

18 Issenberg, 314.

19 The study can be found at: http://www.pewtrusts.org/en/research-and-analysis/issue-briefs/2017/06/why-are-millions-of-citizens-not-registered.

20 William T. Murphy, Jr. and Edward Schneier, *Vote Power: How to Work for the Person You Want Elected* (Garden City, NY: Anchor Books, 1974), 107.

21 Heath Brown, *Immigrants and Electoral Politics: Nonprofit Organizing in a Time of Demographic Change* (Ithaca, NY: Cornell University Press, 2016), 2.

22 Center for Responsive Politics, "Blue Team Aided by Small Donors, Big Bundlers; Huge Outside Spending Still Comes Up Short," November 7, 2012, www.opensecrets.org.

23 Catherine Shaw, *The Campaign Manager: Running and Winning Local Elections* (Bouldeer, CO: Westview Press, fifth ed., 2014), 114.

24 Jeffrey Gildenhorn as quoted in Shaw, 121.

25 Jeff Milyo, "Campaign Spending and Electoral Competition: Towards More Policy Relevant Research," *The Forum: A Journal of Applied Research in Contemporary Politics*, (2013), 37.

26 Theodore J. Eismeier and Philip H. Pollock III, "Money in the 1994 Elections and Beyond," in Philip A. Klinker, ed., *The*

Elections of 1994 in Context (Boulder, CO: Westview Press, 1996), 95.

27 Issenberg, 248.

28 Ibid.

29 Victoria Carty, *Wired and Mobilizing: Social Movements, New Technology and Electoral Politics* (New York: Routledge, 2010).

30 Daniel Kreiss, *Taking Our Country Back: The Crafting of Networked Politics from Howard Dean to Barack Obama* (New York: Oxford University Press, 2012), 195.

31 Murphy and Schneier, 66.

32 Issenberg, 102.

33 Conor M. Dowling and Michael G. Miller, eds., *Super PAC! Money, Elections and Voters After Citizens United* (New York: Routledge, 2014), 7.

34 Donald P. Green and Alan S. Gerber, *Get Out the Vote: How to Increase Voter Turnout* (Washington: The Brookings Institution, 3rd ed., 2015), 9.

35 Robert K. Goidel, Donald A. Gross and Todd G. Shields, *Money Matters: Consequences of Campaign Reform in U. S. House Races* (Lanham, MD: Rowman and Littlefield, 1999), 135-36.

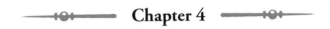

Chapter 4

Advocacy

1. Elections, Agitation and Lobbying

Every legislative campaign should have people working on issues, in the form of opposition research that looks, on the one hand, at where other candidates (incumbents in particular) stand; and, on the other hand, at what positions are best defined and explained in terms of good public policy, good politics, and feasibility. The steps that campaign volunteers can take in helping candidates win can become the first steps in longer range advocacy efforts. Among campaign volunteers, one will almost invariably find a surprising range of policy "experts:" teachers with strong ideas on educational issues, health care workers who understand how the system can be improved, highway workers and maintenance people with ideas on infrastructure. Going to local experts—school superintendents, small business people, drug and alcohol counselors, union leaders, health care professionals, and so on— can be both informative and a useful way of campaigning. People rather like to talk about themselves and what they are doing.

It is in their perceptions of the role of issues in campaigns that volunteers and professionals are most likely to conflict. Professionals view issues more as tools than ends in themselves. It is not that they want candidates to lie or say things they don't mean, but their focus is on deciding questions of tone and emphasis almost entirely in terms of their electoral impact. The signs saying, "It's the economy stupid" that hung on every wall in Bill Clinton's campaign for President were there to remind the candidate and everyone working for him of the importance of staying on message. This can be difficult for many activists to accept. The person who volunteers to work for a candidate largely out of a concern for, say, immigration issues will likely find the campaign's downplaying of those issues a bitter pill to swallow. Yet if all the polls, the focus groups, and the feedback from canvassing show that other issues are the ones resonating with voters, you better be prepared to take the pill. Electing candidates who share your views is the goal, not how they do it.

It is almost certainly a concern about issues that led you to read this book. But as important as issues are in campaigns and elections, issue advocacy is not the same as campaigning. Campaigns are about changing the people who govern, advocacy is about changing their ideas. Certainly there is overlap. When I was an officer of the Princeton Community Democratic Organization in the 1960s we refused to endorse a candidate for the County Board of Chosen Freeholders because he refused to say he opposed the war in Viet Nam. What the hell does the war have to do with county government? he asked. It goes to character, was the best I could reply. I still believe that our stand served a political end: indeed within a year our newly elected Freeholder changed his position on the War as opinion more generally shifted.

A decade later, long before its time, the Downtown Independent Democrats (DID) in lower Manhattan voted not to endorse any candidate who opposed gay rights. I think it made a difference in our liberal district and in the liberal borough of Manhattan; but our position was much less sustainable when it came to city and state-wide elections where few candidates had even thought about the issue. We could and did raise it with them, and that was important; but how could we remain neutral even in our own congressional district when a progressive candidate, who was with us on every other issue, refused to accept our stand on gay rights (which his opponent was even more actively against)? We changed our policy. There are times for agitation and times for pragmatism. Different groups and different individuals will draw the line at different times and on different issues. On the War in the 1970s, the nation was at a turning point. The problem, we thought, was to swing the entire direction of national debate, to shape, in particular, the position of the Democratic Party. On gay rights, the problem was not yet one of mass mobilization or national debate– we hoped that would come in the future– but of simply getting the issue on the political agenda. We were in effect starting the conversation on what turned out to be a decades long, and by no means finished battle. But in that particular time and place, when a major policy shift on the issue was unlikely, it made no sense to abandon whatever influence we might have had on other issues.

Agitation is a strategy not an end. There are times and issues, too long ignored, that need to brought to the forefront. Nationally, it is important to keep progressive dialogue alive and to use the period leading up to 2020 to refine and seek consensus on issues like health care and the environment. If these issues are not ready for prime time in the electoral arena (neither was frequently mentioned in the 2016 campaign), they need to be moved front and center in the broader court of public opinion. What the Democrats can do between 2018 and 2020 is to keep raising these issues as they move toward a consensus on concrete policy proposals that will shape the agenda for debate in 2020. Both as candidates in 2018, and, more importantly, as incumbents in 2019-20, Democratic members of Congress can contrast themselves with today's Republicans by welcoming town hall meetings and legislative hearings openly to discuss these issues. Whether a Democratic President and Congress ultimately agree on Medicare for all, something like the Canadien system, or some other single-payer plan, the dialogue on the left must be civil and focused on, at the very least, retaining and hopefully extending the very real gains of the Obama years. What it must not be is an intolerant attempt to impose an ideology on all Democratic candidates in fifty diverse states.

Agitation is not the same as lobbying. In the 1970s we had no concrete plan as to how we would extract the nation from the War. Even in liberal Manhattan forty years ago, we were talking about discrimination not gay marriage, or the rights of the transgendered. The whole point of agitation is more one of raising questions than of providing answers. That's what lobbyists do. The goal of advocacy is to shape the political agenda, to establish in general terms the issues to be considered and the problems to be debated. Lobbying deals with specific solutions to those issues and seeks to influence the decisions of those in positions of power.

2018 is not a year for progressive lobbying. Whether Democrats can win a majority in the House and score a more improbable upset in the Senate, there will still be a conservative line-up in Washington. To those whose energy is directed toward a single-payer system, or combating climate change, the short run answer is: we lose. Even if Democrats win slender majorities in both the House and Senate, it takes only forty-one votes in the Senate to sustain a filibuster. And even if some moderate Republicans go along, it takes a two-thirds majority to override a presidential veto. We lose. Significant change is not going to come absent major Democratic victories in *both* 2018 and 2020. Except at the state and local level, in other words, progressive issue advocates must think in terms agitation and education *plus* electability. The specifics will come later.

2. The Party System and the Pressure System

In his classic textbook on American politics, V. O. Key defined pressure groups as groups that "promote their interests by attempting to influence government rather than by nominating candidates and seeking responsibility for the management of government."[1] The pressure system, by this definition was narrowly focused both in membership and goals. Parties, conversely sought public support with the goal of winning elections. As a rule, lobbyists worked on the margins of issues, tweaking broad policies in the often narrow interests of their members. Party politicians were seldom involved in the details of policy, often relying in fact on lobbyists to fill them in. The general outlines of this distinction have become increasingly blurred as the parties– Republicans in particular– have become increasingly ideological. The perversity of this blurring was starkly illustrated in the 2017 efforts to repeal the Affordable Care Act.

Under traditional rules of the game, as noted in chapter one, the Republicans would have presented their repeal and replace effort in the form of a bill referred to the relevant committees. As the committees held hearings, various groups representing health insurance companies, hospitals, seniors, pharmaceutical companies and so on would have testified in public and worked to modify various parts of the law. The bill would have been amended and refined as it moved through the committees of each house and through the leadership to the floor. Instead, the bill(s) were drafted in private and presented in a closed package. When the first effort failed, a second was prepared, again without the advice or arguments of the affected groups, but solely in a search for more Republican support. When that failed, there was yet a third iteration of same process. Despite the substantive differences between them, 47 Republican Senators indicated support for all three bills. What they were in effect saying was something like this:

Do you support the idea that health insurance providers should not be able to deny coverage to people with pre-existing conditions? Yes I supported legislation to do that.

Do you support legislation that allows health insurance providers to deny coverage to people with pre-existing conditions? Yes, I supported legislation to do that.

Do you support leaving the question of pre-existing conditions to the states? Yes I supported that. The same bizarre story was essentially repeated in the House.

Each of the 2017 health care bills was, to be sure, complicated, and each contained issues other than coverage for people with pre-existing conditions. In the "normal" course of the legislative process, these complications would have been worked out through a series of compromises in which the rules on this part of the health care act would have been balanced against each other. Here, however, all that mattered was the majority party's promise to repeal and replace Obamacare. With what? No matter. How? No matter. With who's council and advice? No matter. In the brave new world of a new political order, symbols displace substance, campaign politics replace legislative processes, and ideology trumps rationality. This is a world, not of Aristotelean logic but of Orwellian double- (make that triple-) speak that threatens seriously to subvert some of the most basic principles of our constitutional system. And then, as if compound the felony, the tax reform bill was crafted in much the same behind-the-curtains, top-down fashion.

The old system was not without serious flaws. What is often called "Madisonian pluralism," from James Madison's brilliant defense of group politics in the *Federalist Papers,* was never as balanced and open a system of give-and-take as it was cracked up to be. Virtually every recent study of interest groups in America concludes that the pressure system has an upper-class bias, with business groups particularly over-represented.[2] While some of the work of interest groups took place behind closed doors and– particularly since the Supreme Court opened the doors to virtually unlimited and untraceable campaign contributions– much of the Washington work of lobbyists remained relatively transparent. Most businesses and organizations wanted, and still want, tangible evidence that their investment in a lobbyist was worthwhile. They preferred to see testimony before committees, position papers, and actual records of visits to legislators to quiet assurances from their hired hands that "we have been working behind the scenes." With bills like the repeal and replace health program and the 2017 tax "reform" proposals there is no such transparency, and– perhaps more importantly– none of the expert if biased public vetting of the opinions of affected groups.

The original Affordable Care Act, as we have noted, was not a model of transparency and due process; but the contrast with "repeal and replace" is in some ways exemplary of two different models of the how interest group politics works. In the original fight, the organized forces fighting over health care issues in Washington were diverse and to a considerable degree balanced. Major players included health insurance companies, the American Medical Association and groups representing practitioners of various medical specialties, labor unions, state governments, hospitals, groups advocating for particular health threats such as cancer, large employers and the American Association of Retired People. The conflicts between and among them are informatively transparent. To be sure, there were two major flaws in the representational profile of the groups struggle: the big pharmaceutical companies, on the one hand, were clearly major players and the general public generally under-represented.

But contrast this with "repeal and replace." Since the House and Senate bills were drafted (and revised) in secret one-party meetings, we have no tangible information on what interest groups were involved. The circumstantial evidence, however, strongly suggests that the pharmaceutical companies were alone among the usual groups involved in consideration of health care issues. They were alone among all the usual players in health care politics who did not react with surprise and opposition to the bills as they emerged; and in contrast with other groups, their campaign contributions to members of the drafting teams increased dramatically. Most importantly, despite an angry public, presidential rhetoric, and numerous, sometimes bi-partisan efforts in Congress to control drug prices, none of these were reflected in any of the repeal and replace bills.[3]

This kind of off-stage, partisan lobbying is what Madison and the founders feared. Trying to check direct democracy– the kind recently referred to as populism– they constructed a system that emphasized checks and balances, numerous access points, and institutional arrangements that made bargaining and compromise essential. If this system makes government "inefficient" in some senses, it forces open debate and alternative points of view. When interest groups know that their arguments will be weighed against those of others, they make their best case in the hope that by weighing opposing arguments sound public policies emerge. A starting point for restoring and transparency back into our politics is to build pluralism into campaign 2018. To put people back into politics is to put associations back as well, to promote candidates who cultivate expertise instead of taking their orders from the large donors or national party leaders. Restoring a viable pluralism and bringing rationality back into politics depends in part on electing representatives who have a genuine interest in policy issues and whose base of support is at the grassroots.

3. The Changing Scope and Bias of the Pressure System

As with electoral politics, the key to balancing the upper class bias of the pressure system is to develop a more viable pluralism: that is, to put people back into pressure politics. This is particularly important for liberals who, with the decline of organized labor, are losing their most significant voice in Washington and in most states. Using the leverage given them by the changing campaign finance rules, a small group of very wealthy donors have became so crucial to congressional Republicans that they virtually control major aspects of Republican policy. And the Democrats are moving in that direction. The large independent political action committees, whose spending is generally skewed to the right, are now generally estimated to spend more money anonymously on campaigns than all regulated donors combined. Even among the financial supporters of both parties that can be identified, almost half of the money donated comes from a tiny handful of very large donors who collectively account for as much as two-thirds of all campaign funds. To the extent that Big Pharma was the only health interest in the room when repeal and replace was being put together, so it appears were the House and Senate tax "reforms" crafted with only a small slice of the business community in the room. Interestingly, the number of organized groups with advocacy offices in Washington, which had been growing for more than a century, has actually declined by more than thirty percent since 2006.[4] As popular as it is for politicians and pundits to rail against "special interests," by which they mean lobbyists, they are doing so at a time when these groups are fading from power. Certainly, few Washington lobbyists face imminent unemployment, but with Republicans in power they are, ironically, increasingly marginal to a legislative process increasingly dominated by the largest and most affluent of all special interests. A recent book by Matt Grossman and David Hopkins argues that the nature of the two parties are increasingly asymmetric. "While the Democratic Party is fundamentally a group coalition, the Republican Party can be most accurately characterized as the vehicle of an ideological movement."[5] The core Republican principle favoring less government, particularly at the national level, resonates well with voters, but the specific policy proposals that flow from it do not. Indeed Republican success at the polls has derived almost entirely from perceptions of what they are against. While Democrats are often criticized for not having a unifying ideology, their positions on specific issues tend to have broad popular support. It makes sense, in this context, to play to strength rather than weakness, to hit the Republicans not with a losing appeal for big government (as it would be portrayed), but with calls for defending and expanding specific programs already having widespread approval such as Medicare, renewable energy, bank regulation, public education, and so on.

Effective advocacy on these and other issues runs along two tracks. In the short run, there are always openings for influence on narrow issues: seeking a legislator's help in finding sources of funding for a local library, protesting the proposed route of a pipeline, making sure that the research budget for health continues to include a specific rare disease. On larger issues, the key is to deconstruct the Republican ideology, to show how cuts and changes in programs affect real people. The goal of what I call agitation is two-fold, on the one hand, as was shown in the failed attempts to repeal and replace Obamacare, the hundreds of thousands of people who turned out to focus on the real effects of specific aspects of the bills probably helped to bring about its defeat(s). Of even more importance were the effects of these efforts on consolidating opposition forces and changing the agenda of political discourse. This is what the Democratic Club efforts on the War in Viet Nam and gay rights, described earlier in this chapter, sought to do: they didn't end the war, they didn't end discrimination; they did change the terms of discourse. In one of the most insightful political texts ever written, E. E Schattschneider argued that "the definition of alternatives is the supreme instrument of power. . . He who determines what politics is about runs the country, because the definition of alternatives is the choice of conflicts, and the choice of conflicts allocates power."[6] Read that again, because it gets to the essence of what I am trying to say about the two tracks of advocacy. Lobbying, in the narrow sense of trying to change public policy, is effective largely on the margins of major issues, usually quite specialized in its objectives, and aimed directly at office holders rather than voters. Advocacy is not about the specifics of policy. If it is aimed at an office holder, it targets him or her as a symbol: its real target is public opinion.

What this means, in practical terms, is that the techniques and tactics that work for agitators are not particularly useful for lobbyists and vice versa. What about lobbying?

4. Effective Lobbying

As a newly-minted PhD in 1963 I found myself in the heady position of Legislative Assistant to the junior senator from Indiana Birch Bayh. One of my jobs was to prepare a daily memo briefly summarizing the bills likely to come to the floor, together with the positions of major interest groups and my own recommendation. Early in my new job there was a bill from a senator from Wisconsin changing the system for milk marketing quotas. What I knew about milk was that it came from cows. I read the bill and the committee report and, quite frankly, couldn't figure it out. The Agriculture Committee person I talked with was not much help, and the Farmer's Union lobbyist I called was busy. The Senator, as a Democrat, generally preferred the advice of the Farmer's Union to the more conservative Farm Bureau, but Herb Harris of the Bureau was in my office an hour after I called. His lucid explanation of the bill virtually wrote my memo, but his bottom line was a surprise. We're for this bill, he said, but it's not good for Indiana. Your guy should vote against it, and he explained why.

Mr. Harris did not help the Bureau's cause on that bill,

but he became my go-to guy on agricultural issues. And this tells you three very important things about lobbying. First, most members of Congress and their staff people don't think of lobbying as "pressure." Interest groups provide an important service for politicians with an interest in good public policy. My guess is that as many of the contacts between politicians and their staff people, on the one hand, and lobbyists on the other, are initiated by the former. Second, the prime currency of interest group effectiveness is trust. Inside the beltway nothing is more important than credibility, or as one old-time congressman crudely put it: "Snow is for the folks, it don't fly here." Third, lobbying, by and large, is organizational, on-going and informed. Citizen lobbyists are, in effect, triply disadvantaged: lacking in-depth knowledge they have relatively little expertise to provide; lacking a history of relations, it is difficult for them to acquire trust; and lacking an ongoing organizational presence, they are hard to find. But they also have some significant, if too-seldom tapped strengths.

Let us note from the outset that citizen lobbyists, unlike many professionals, seldom have either the financial or research resources that enable professionals to work across district lines. Letters and phone calls from non-constituents are seldom counted or taken seriously. And the angrier they are, the less their credibility. A young lawyer, hired by a very conservative Senator was given— as one of his first chores— the task of answering a pile of letters from all over the country dealing with questions for which the office had no stock answers. After working through most of them, he was left with a small pile accusing the Senator of everything but mass murder. "How do I respond to these?" he asked. "Give them a noncommital answer," the Senator replied. "Well, I figured that, but what specifically should I say?" "Tell them to go fuck themselves," the Senator replied. Some staffers still use the phrase "give them a noncommital answer" as a euphemism for what they really mean.

But citizen lobbyists have advantages too. Most importantly, they know their districts and their local concerns Unlike Herb Harris, moreover, many local citizen lobbyists don't have to earn their legislator's trust: they already have it, as friends, neighbors and, most importantly, as parts of their winning campaigns. "Each member of Congress," Richard Fenno argues, "perceives four concentric constituencies: geographic, reelection, primary and personal."[7] Only a small number of campaign volunteers, if any, work their way into the innermost of these circles, the family members and oldest friends with whom they have both political and emotional connections; but the primary circle, sometimes defined as "the ones each congressman believes would provide his last line of electoral defense in a primary contest"[8] is often comprised largely of volunteers. These are the people who Birch Bayh called the "stand up sons-of-a-bitches," those who when you need volunteers to get a mailing out after hours would mutter "son-of-a-bitch" and stand up to get it done. When these people visited his Washington office, they had as much access to the Senator as his largest campaign contributors. Indeed some recent research suggests that what some academics call "social lobbying," the ability to talk to members in unstructured, informal settings is particularly effective.

Those in what Fenno calls the reelection circle, may not have privileged access, but the door is usually open.

What about active Democrats represented by Republicans (and vice versa)? By and large, they get noncommittal answers, especially when the numbers of letters, phone calls, e-mails and demonstrators are relatively small. These cross-party lobbying efforts can have an impact, however, in the following kinds of ways. It can matter when there are large numbers of people, not all of them known partisans, who seem generally concerned about the negative effects of proposed legislation. This occurred in 2017 in many districts on repeal and replace health care bills where the usual suspects were joined by people not known to be partisans but sincerely concerned about the personal impact of the bills on their lives. When doctors, seniors, people with pre-existing conditions, and so on joined the demonstrations, it made a difference. While few congressional minds were changed, the impact on district opinion was sometimes significant, particularly in districts where representatives openly avoided or dismissed public dialogue. Group efforts on issues of this kind, that is where advocacy moves from lobbying to agitation, can also morph into recruitment opportunities for future electoral activity.

A second kind of effective lobbying across party lines works for people with specific and particular experiences or expertise. A thoughtful letter, especially on an arcane subject, that details a businessperson's experience with a costly but unnecessary regulation, a consumer's experience with an unregulated type of fraud, a former diplomat's tale of mistaken American policies in another country, these are grist for the congressional mill. Even in today' hyper-partisan era, a bi-partisan bill to relieve smaller banks from some of the restrictions imposed by Dodd-Franks seems likely to pass. On narrow issues such as this, the old-fashioned Madisonian system still works. So too, unfortunately, does an equally effective commodity, money– big money that is– cross district lines. The basic' rule of thumb, however, is that politicians look first to their districts, to individuals and groups from inside it, and to national organizations that have substantial numbers of members in the district.

5. Legislative Intelligence

Here are the things legislators, at least those who have some independence from party leaders, want to know: what is the problem seeking solution, what can be done by whom, who will it hurt or help, and how will it play in a future campaign? Members of Congress are overwhelmed with data: literally dozens of reports are generated every week by government agencies, private foundations, state governments, interest groups, journalists and academics, many of them relevant to the work the legislature. Looking at the figures pieced together in one of the leading texts on interest groups in American politics, it can be calculated that the average member of Congress receives roughly 370,000 letter, e-mails, telephone calls and faxes every year, more than a thousand a day.[9] What legislators need are methods of refining, winnowing and making political sense of this data overload. To do this,

> Outside of the areas in which he himself has special knowledge and interest, the legislator needs sources of information which can combine, in one neat package,

an evaluation of a program's significance, popularity, and relationship to other negotiable issue. The most economical form in which such information can be packaged is that which contains the least data. The best information that he [or she] can have on some issues is a reliable directive to vote yes or no.[10]

The tricky part of this is, of course, the word *reliable.* And this is precisely where the citizen lobbyist is particularly advantaged (or disadvantaged, as the case may be) by the simple fact of being a known commodity, known, if not personally, at least by reputation. The better you know your representative and, more importantly, the better he or she knows you, the more probable your access.

Legislators are not beginning with a blank slate. All have a sense of who their consistent supporters are, who are consistent opponents, and who occupy the spaces in between. . . . Most legislators play a conservative game and follow the preferences of their most consistent supporters rather than those of their past opponents.[11]

They play to their base, and pay special attention to those who are known commodities. In many cases, this gives local activists a good part of the credibility that every lobbyist seeks.

Credibility is based on more than just familiarity. Above

all it depends on having useful information in digested form: intelligence, as I like to call it, as opposed to information. It combines processed and evaluated technical information with an understanding of local politics and economic conditions. It includes realism, not asking the legislator to do something that is politically or fiscally impossible– when you ask that you go from providing help to being a pain. It may often include an honest portrayal of opposing arguments, because "good information is important not just for arguing within Congress but also for justifying one's position to constituents." As Levine continues, "As unquestionable as is the congressional thirst for good information, the distaste for bad information is even more pronounced."[12] Building trust begins, at a minimum, with building competence. There is no doubt that a well-organized, well-financed Washington or state lobbying office is tremendously advantaged in both its ability to develop a bank of expert knowledge for officeholders to draw upon, and a continuing availability in the capitol.

In the best case scenario, these lobbying offices are able to mobilize large numbers of members, customers, clients and friends to contact their legislators. The idea is that if, say, all the automobile dealers in a legislator's district write to support a specific bill, their lobbyist is more likely to be able to find a receptive audience when he or she comes to make the case. Many state legislatures have formal advocacy days, organized by professional lobbyists, where hundreds of gun owners, college students and faculty, senior citizens, hikers, small business owners and union members roam the halls visiting their local State Senators and Assembly members to, in effect, soften them up for a more detailed and professional presentation.

For political activists, the point of grassroots campaigns goes beyond such short-term goals. First, in terms of the case made in this book for putting people back in politics, it is part of a longer range strategy to build a movement for change. Just as professional campaign managers play an important role in elections, but are vastly more effective when joined with citizen activists, so are professional lobbyists strengthened by their links to involved constituents. Second, rallying around issues is an effective vehicle for sustaining a campaign organization between elections and forging new alliances. And finally there are (fortunately) a number of voters who really do care about issues and who want to be represented by legislators who do. So even if many (if not most) Republican incumbents play follow the leader and have little use for expert opinion, there are good reasons to establish advocacy groups, to engage in issues research, and at least go through the motions of lobbying.

Grassroots lobbying is only as effective as its follow-up. A California Congressman Clem Miller once compared two groups– walnut growers and chicken farmers– who had lobbying days in Washington. The walnut growers, though far less numerous than the poultry people, got pretty much what they wanted, the chicken farmers nothing. The difference was that the walnut group hired a lobbyist to follow up on their visit. He or she sent a follow-up letter to each of the legislators the farmers had visited and then visited their offices with a specific plan of action. The good will generated by the chicken farmers, conversely, faded away as they went home, leaving it up to the Congressmen to initiate a policy. No matter how good the cause, getting legislators to pay attention to your issue is not easy: the chicken farmers lost not because of active opposition but because the congressmen they contacted had more pressing concerns. It helps, of course, to have a paid professional to do this follow up work; but there is no reason that dedicated volunteers, in lobbying as in campaigning cannot shoulder much of the burden.

6. People Power

The road back toward a more rational, reasoned and compassionate polity is long. It is made all the more difficult by a widespread and growing mistrust of government, science and expertise in general. Fueled munificently by a handful of ideological fanatics hiding behind the destruction of campaign finance regulations, the radical rich are well on the way to destroying democracy as we know it. We can write checks to decent candidates and if enough of us do, we might be able partially to match the tens of millions given each year by a large network of similar big donors, but the gap is huge.[13] We are learning, moreover, that in an ideological battle between those favoring the abstraction of more government rather than less, Democrats lose. Democrats win when they shift attention to concrete issues and the real problems of real people. They can win too, as I have argued, when they put people back into politics shifting the locus of campaigns from wholesale to retail and putting a human face on the message.

The radical labor organizer Joe Hill asked on his death bed that his followers "don't mourn for me, organize." We must do the same. Whether the task is campaigns and elections, agitation or lobbying, organization is what makes it work in the long run. And it will be a long run. No matter how well progressive forces do in the 2018 midterm elections, the wahoos will still have veto power. And to roll back the gerrymanders, restrictions on voting rights and campaign finance rules that so distort majority rule will take years. And it may be years beyond that before the American people have confidence enough in themselves to restore their faith in democratic government. John F. Kennedy was fond of the Chinese proverb that the longest journey begins with a single step. Tis is the year to take that step.

Endnotes

1   V. O. Key, *Politics, Parties, and Pressure Groups* (New York: Alfred A. Knopf, 4th ed., 1998), 23.

2   See, for example, Lee Drutman, *The Business of America is Lobbying: How Corporations Became Politicized and Politics Became More Corporate* (New York: Oxford University Press, 2015).

3   Jay Hancock, "Big Pharma Can't Lose," The New York *Times,* September 24, 2017, F7.

4   The Center for Responsive Politics has been tracking these numbers for twenty years. Because they count only those who have actually registered under the law, their figures are generally thought to be lower than the number of groups that occasionally contact government officials.

5   Matt Grossman and David A. Hopkins, *Asymmetric Politics: Ideological Republicans and Group Interest Democrats* (New York: Oxford University Press, 2016), 3.

6   E. E. Schattsneider, *The Semisovereign People: A Realists View of Democracy in America* (New York: Holt, Rinehart and Winston, 1960), 68.

7   Richard F. Fenno, Jr., *Home Style: House Members in Their Districts* (Boston: Little, Brown, 1978), 27

8   Ibid., 18.

9   Anthony J. Nownes, *Interest Groups in American Politics: Pressure and Power* (New York: Routledge, 2nd ed., 2013), 175.

10 Edward Schneier, "The Intelligence of Congress: Information and Public-Policy Patterns," 388 *Annals of the American Academy of Political and Social Science* (March 1970), 18.

11 R. Douglas Arnold, *The Logic of Congressional Action* (New Haven: Yale University Press, 1990), 83.

12 Bertram J. Levine, *The Art of Lobbying: Building Trust and Selling Policy* (Washington: CQ Press, 2009), 135.

13 Jane Mayer, *Dark Money: The Hidden History of the Billionaires Behind the Rise of the Radical Right* (New York: Doubleday, 2016).

Appendix A: The Eighty-one Most Marginal House Districts in 2018

State and District	2016 Results	2014 Results	Presidential Margin in 2016	Rating	Targeted
Alaska AL	R: Young 50.3 D: Lindbeck 36.1	R: Young 51.6 D: Dunbar 40.8	R +15.2	Leans R	
Arizona 1	D: O'Halleran 50.8 R: Babeu 43.5	D: Kirkpatrick 52.6 R: Tobin 47.4	R +1.1	Leans D	DC, RC
Arizona 2	R: McSally 56.7* D: Heinz 43.3	R: McSally 50.0 D: Barber 50.0	D +4.9	Leans D	DC
Arizona 9	D: Sinema 60.9* R: Giles 39.0	D: Sinema 54.7 R: Rogers 41.9	D +19.1	Likely D	RC
California 7	D: Bera 51.2 R: Jones 48.8	D: Bera 50.4 R: Ose 49.6	D +11.4	Leans D	DC, RC
California 10	R: Denham 51.7 D: Eggman	R: Denham 56.1 D: Eggman 43.9	D +3.0	Leans R	DC
California 21	R: Valadao 56.7 D: Huerta 43.3	R: Valadao 57.8 D: Renteria 42.2	D +25.8	Likely R	DC, RC
California 24	D: Carbajal 53.4 R: Fared 46.6	D: Capps 51.9 R: Mitchum 48.1	D +20.2	Likely D	DC, RC
California 25	R: Knight 53.1 D: Caforio 46.9	R: Knight 53.3 No Democrat	D +6.7	Toss-up	DC, RC
California 39	R: Royce 57.2* D: Murdock 42.8	R: Royce 68.5 D: Anderson 31.5	D +8.6	Toss-up	DC

District					
California 45	R: Walters 58.6 D: Varasteh 41.4	R: Walters 65.1 D: Leavens 34.9	D +5.4	Leans R	DC
California 48	R: Rohrabacher 58.3 D: Savary 41.7	R: Rohrabacher 64.1 D: Savary 35.9	D +1.7	Toss-up	DC
California 49	R: Issa 51.0* D: Applegate 49.0	R: Issa 60.2 D: Peiser 39.8	D +7.5	Leans D	DC, RC
California 50	R: Hunter 63.5 D: Malloy 36.5	R: Hunter 71.2 D: Kimber 28.8	R +15	Likely R	
Colorado 6	R: Coffman 50.9 D: Carroll 42.6	R: Coffman 51.9 D: Romanoff 43.0	D +8.9	Toss-up	DC
Florida 7	D: Murphy 51.5 R: Mica 48.5	R: Mica 63.6 D: Neuman 32.1	D +7.3	Leans D	DC, RC
Florida 13	D: Crist 51.9 R: Jolly 48.1	R: Jolly 75.2 No Democrat	D +3.2	Likely D	DC, RC
Florida 18	R: Mast 53.6 D: Perkins 43.1	D: Murphy 59.8 R: Domino 38.4	R +9.2	Likely R	DC, RC
Florida 26	R: Curbelo 53.0 D: Garcia 41.2	R: Curbelo 51.5 D: Garcia 48.5	R +16.3	Toss-up	DC
Florida 27	R: R-Lehtinen 54.9* D: Fuhrman 45.1	R: R-Lehtinen 100 No Democrat	R +19.6	Leans D	DC, RC
Georgia 6	See note 1	R: R: Price 66 D: Montigel 34	R +1.5	Leans R	DC, RC
Illinois 6	R: Roskam 59.2 D: Howland 40.8	R: Roskam 67.1 D: Mason 32.9	D +7.0	Likely R	DC, RC

Illinois 12	R: Bost 54.3 D: Baricevic 39.7	R: Bost 52.5 D: Enyart 41.9	R +14.8	Leans R	
Illinois 13	R: Davis 59.7 D: Wicklund 40.3	R: Davis 58.6 D: Callis 41.3	R +5.5	Likely R	DC
Illinois 14	R: Hullgren 59.3 D: Walz 40.7	R: Hultgren 59.6 D: Walz 40.4	R +3.9	Likely R	DC
Iowa 1	R: Blum 53.8 D: Vernon 46.2	R: Blum 51.1 D: Murphy 48.8	R +3.5	Leans R	DC
Iowa 2	D: Loebsack 53.7 R: Peters 46.3	D: Loebsack 52.5 R: Mil'r-Meeks 49.4	R +4.1	Likely D	DC, RC
Iowa 3	R: Young 53.5 D: Mowrer 39.8	R: Young 52.8 D: Appel 42.2	R +3.5	Likely R	DC
Kansas 2	R: Jenkins 60.9* D: Potter 32.5	R: Jenkins 61.1 D: Wakefield 38.6	R +18.4	Leans R	DC, RC
Kansas 3	R: Yoder 51.3 D: Sidie 40.6	R: Yoder 60.2 D: Kultala 39.8	D +1.2	Leans R	DC
Kentucky 6	R: Barr 61.1 D: Kemper 38.9	R: Barr 60.0 D: Jensen 40.0	R +15.3	Likely R	DC
Maine 2	R: Poliquin 54.9 D: Cain 45.1	R: Poliquin 47.0 D: Cain 41.8	R +10.3	Leans R	DC
Michigan 8	R: Bishop 56.0 D: Shkreli 39.2	R: Bishop 54.6 D: Schertzing 42.1	R +6.7	Leans R	DC
Michigan 11	R: Trott 52.9 D: Kumar 40.2	R: Trott 55.9 D: McKenzie 40.5	R +4.44	Toss-up	DC, RC

Minnesota 1	D: Walz 50.4 R: Hagedorn 49.6	D: Walz 54.2 R: Hagedorn 45.7	R +14.9	Toss-up	DC, RC
Minnesota 2	R: Lewis 47.2 D: Craig 45.2	R: Kline 56.0 D: Obermueller 38.9	R +1.2	Toss-up	DC, RC
Minnesota 3	R: Paulsen 56.9 D: Bonoff 43.1	R: Paulsen 62.1 D: Sund 37.8	R +9.4	Leans R	DC
Minnesota 7	D: Peterson 52.5 R: Hughes 47.5	D: Peterson 54.2 R: Westrom 45.6	R + 30.8	Likely D	RC
Minnesota 8	D: Nolan 50.3* R: Mills 49.7	D: Nolan 48.5 R: Mills 47.1	D +7.8	Toss-up	DC, RC
Montana AL	See note 2	R: Zinke 55.4 D: Lewis 40.4	R +20.6	Likely R	
Nebraska 2	R: Bacon 49.4 D: Ashford 47.3	D: Ashford 48.9 R: Terry 45.6	R +2.2	Toss-up	DC
Nevada 3	D: Rosen 47.2 R: Tarkanian 46.0	R: Heck 60.8 D: Bilbray 36.1	R +1.0	Toss-up	DC, RC
Nevada 4	D: Kilhuen 48.5 R: Hardy 44.5	R: Hardy 63.5 D: Horsford 45.8	D +4.9	Lean D	DC, RC
N Hampshire 1	D: Shea-Porter 44.2* R: Guinta 42.9	R: Guinta 49.0 D: Shea_Porter 48.1	R +1.6	Toss-up	DC, RC
N Hampshire 2	D: Kuster 49.8 R: Lawrence 45.4	D: Kuster 54.8 R: Garcia 44.9	D +2.4	Likely D	DC, RC
New Jersey 2	R: LoBiondi 59.4* D: Cole 37.1	R: LoBiondo 61.5 D: Hughes 37.3	R +4.6	Toss-up	DC

New Jersey 3	R: MacArthur 59.5 D: LaVergne 38.6	R: MacArthur 54.0 D: Belgard 44.4	R +6.6	Likely R	DC
New Jersey 5	D: Gottheimer 50.5 R: Garrett 47.2	R: Garrett 55.4 D: Cho 43.3	R +1.1	Leans D	DC, RC
New Jersey 7	R: Lance 54.2 D: Jacob 43.0	R: Lance 59.2 D: Kovach 38.7	D +1.1	Leans R	DC
New Jersey 11	R: Fre'husen 58.2* D: Wenzel 38.7	R: Fre'husen 62.6 D: Dunec 37.4	R +.9	Leans R	DC
New Mexico 2	R: Pearce 62.7 D: Soules 37.3	R: Pearce 64.3 D: Lara 35.5	R +10.2	Likely R	RC
New York 1	R: Zeldin 59.0 D: Thr'-Holst 41.0	R: Zeldin 54.4 D: Bishop 45.5	R +12.3	Likely R	DC
New York 3	D: Suozzi 52.4 R: Martins 47.6	D: Israel 54.7 R: Lally 45.2	D +6.1	Likely D	DC, RC
New York 11	R: Donovan 62.2 D: Reichard 36.1	R: Grimm 54.8 D: Recchia 42.1	R +9.8	Likely R	DC
New York 18	D: Maloney 55.6 R: Oliva 44.4	D: Maloney 49.7 R: Hayworth 47.8	R +1.9	Likely D	DC, RC
New York 19	R: Faso 54.7 D: Teachout 45.3	R: Gibson 64.5 D: Eldridge 35.5	R +6.8	Toss-up	DC, RC
New York 22	R: Tenney 47.2 D: Myers 40.4	R: Hanna 98.4 Unopposed	R +15.5	Leans R	DC, RC
New York 24	R: Katco 61.0 D: Deacon 39.0	R: Katko 59.5 D: Maffei 40.3	D +3.6	Likely R	DC

N. Carolina 2	R: Holding 56.7 D: McNiel 43.3	R: Ellmers 58.8 D: Aiken 41.2	R +9.6	Likely R	
N. Carolina 9	R: Pittinger 58.3 D: Cano 41.7	R: Pittinger 93.9 Unopposed	R +11.6	Likely R	DCCC
N. Carolina 13	R: Budd 56.1 D: Davis 43.9	R: Holding 57.3 D: Cleary 42.7	R +9.4	Likely R	DC, RC
Ohio 1	R: Chabot 59.6 D: Young 50.4	R: Chabot 63.2 D: Kundrata 36.8	R +6.6	Likely R	DC
Ohio 12	R: Tiberi 66.6* D: Albertson 29.8	R: Tiberi 68.1 D: Tibbs 27.8	R +11.3	Likely R	DC
Pennsylvania 6	R: Costello 57.3 D: Parrish 42.7	R: Costello 56.3 D: Trivedi 43.7	D +.6	Leans R	DC
Pennsylvania 7	R: Meehan 59.7* D: Balchunis 40.3	R: Meehan 62.0 D: Balchunis 37.9	D +2.3	Leans R	DC
Pennsylvania 8	R: Fitzpatrick 54.5 D: Santarsiero 45.5	R: Fitzpatrick 61.9 D: Strouse 38.1	D +.2	Leans R	DC, RC
Pennsylvania 15	R: Dent 58.4* D: Daugherty 38.0	R: Dent 100. Unopposed	R +7.6	Leans R	DC
Pennsylvania 16	R: Smucker 53.9 D: Hartman 42.7	R: Pitts 57.7 D: Houghton 42.3	R +6.8	Leans R	DC
Pennsylvania 17	D: Cartwright 53.8 R: Connolly 46.2	D: Cartwright 56.8 R: Moylan 43.2	R +10.1	Likely D	RC
Pennsylvania 18	See Note 3	R: Murphy 100	R +0.7	Likely R	

Texas 7	R: Culberson 56.2 D: Cargas 43.8	R: Culberson 63.3 D: Cargas 34.6	D +1.4	Likely R	
Texas 23	R: Hurd 48.5 D: Gallego 46.8	R: Hurd 49.8 D: Gallego 47.7	D +3.4	Toss-up	DC, RC
Texas 32	R: Sessions 71.1 No Democrat	R: Sessions 63.6 D: Perez 35.4	D +1.9	Likely R	DC, RC
Utah 4	R: Love 53.5 D: Owens 41.7	R: Love 50.9 D: Owens 45.8	R +6.7	Likely R	DC
Virginia 2	R: Taylor 61.7 D: Brown 38.3	R: Rigell 58.7 D: Patrick 41.1	R +3.4	Likely R	DC
Virginia 5	R: Garrett 58.3 D: Dittmar 41.7	R: Hurt 60.9 D: Gaughan 35.8	R +11.1	Likely R	
Virginia 7	R: Brat 57.5 D: Bedell 42.2	R: Brat 60.8 D: Trammell 36.9	R +6.5	Likely R	
Virginia 10	R: Comstock 52.9 D: Bennett 47.1	R: Comstock 56.5 D: Foust 40.4	D +10.0	Toss-up	DC, RC
Washington 8	R: Reichert 60.0* D: Ventrella 40.0	R: Reichert 63.3 D: Ritchie 36.7	D +3.0	Toss-up	DC, RC
Wisconsin 3	D: Kind 100 Unopposed	D: Kind 56.5 R: Kurtz 43.4	R +4.5	Likely D	RC
Wisconsin 6	R: Grothman 57.2 D: Lloyd 37.3	R: Grtothman 56.8 D: Harris 40.9	R + 15.9	Likely R	DC

*Indicates an incumbent who has retired or indicated that he or she will not run for re-election in 2018.

Note 1: Georgia's 6th District became vacant when the incumbent Republican resigned. A special election to fill the vacancy in this normally safe-Republican district saw newcomer Jon Ossoff come within fewer than 10,000 votes of a major upset. The new incumbent, Congresswoman Karen Handel is running for re-election, and although Jon Ossoff apparently is not, Democrats have targeted the district as one they can flip in 2018.

Note 2: This is another case of a special election in a normally Republican district that came out closer than expected. Republican Greg Gianforte, who gained 50% of the vote compared to Rob Quist's 44.4%, is running for re-election in 2018. There will be a primary election in election in June to choose a Democrat to run against Gianforte who may have made himself more vulnerable by allegedly assaulting a reporter at the conclusion of his 2017 campaign.

Note 3: Although Congressman Murphy appeared to be a safe bet for re-election in 2018, his resignation in the wake of a sex scandal has resulted in a March 2018 special election that could be very close in a district in which the two parties have generally been competitive.

Sources and Key: Throughout 2017 a number of organizations tracked the 2018 campaigns for the House of Representatives rating them on a five-point scale of likely outcomes. Although they use different labels and slightly different calculations, districts are generally characterized as either "safe" for one party or the other, "likely" Republican or Democratic, "leaning," or too close to call ("toss up"). This table presents the major party results of the 2014 and 2016

House elections together with the average rankings of three political observers, the Cook Report, Inside Elections and Larry Sabato's Crystal Ball, and frequent analyses reported in Politico and the New York Times. The eighty-nine races listed here are those not rated safe for one party or the other. The column on the right of the Table indicates whether the National or Congressional Campaign Committees of the Republican and Democratic Parties have targeted each district. Most of the numbers reported here are taken from various reports of Ballotpedia, an absolutely invaluable source of data for those interested in elections.

Appendix B: Nineteen Possibly Marginal House Districts

Alabama 2	R: Roby 54.6 D: Mathis 45.4	R: Roby 66.1 D: Wright 33.9	R +31.9	Safe R	DC
California 16	D: Costa 58.0 R: Tacherra 42.0	D: Costa 50.7 R: Tacherra 49.3	D +21.6	Safe D	
Colorado 3	R: Tipton 54.6 D: Schwartz 40.3	R: Tipton 58 D: Tapia 35.7	R +12	Safe R	DC
Florida 25	R: Diaz-Balart 62.4 D: Valdes 37.6	R: Diaz-Balart unopposed	R +1.8	Safe R	DC
Georgia 7	R: Woodall 60.4 D: Malik 39.6	R: Woodall 65.4 D: Wight 34.6	R +6.3	Safe R	
Illinois 10	D: Schneider 52.6 R: Dold 47.4	R: Dold 51.3 D: Schneider 48.7	D +19.4	Safe D	DC, RC
Illinois 17	D: Bustos 60.3 R: Harlan 39.7	D: Bustos 55.5 R: Schilling 44.5	R +0.7	Safe D	DC, RC
Indiana 9	R: Hollingsworth 54.1 D: Yoder 40.5	R: Young 62.2 D: Bailey 33.7	R +25.9	Safe R	DC
Michigan 7	R: Walberg 55.1 D: Driskell 40.0	R: Walberg 53.4 D: Byrnes 41.2	R +17	Safe R	DC
New York 21	R: Stefanik 65. D: Derrick 30.2	R: Stefanik 53 D: Woolf 32.5	R +13.9	Safe R	
New York 23	R: Reed 58.1 D: Plumb 41.9	R: Reed 61.7 D: Robertson 38.3	R +14.8	Safe R	

N. Carolina 2	R: Holding 56.7	R: Ellmers 58.8	R +9.6	Safe R	
	D: McNell 43.3	D: Aiken 41.2			
N. Carolina 13	R: Budd 56.1	R: Holding 57.3	R +9.4	Safe R	DC
	D: Davis 43.9	D: Cleary 42.7			
Ohio 16	R: Renacci 65.3	R: Renacci 63.7	R +16.6	Safe R	
	D: Mundy 34.7	D: Crossland 36.3			
Oregon 5	D: Schrader 53.6	D: Blumenauer 72.3	D +4.2	Safe D	RC
	R: Willis 43.2	R: Buchal 19.6			
Texas 21	R: Smith 57*	R: Smith 71.8	R +7.9	Safe R	DC
	D: Wakely 36.4	D: Diaz 14.7			
Virginia 7	R: Brat 57.9	R: Brat 60.8	R +6.5	Safe R	
	D: Bedell 42.1	D: Trammell 36.9			
Washington 5	R: Rodgers 59.6	R: Rodgers 60.7	R +13.1	Safe R	DC
	D: Pakoottas 40.4	D: Pakootas 39.3			
W. Virginia 3	R: Jenkins 67.9*	R: Jenkins 55.4	R + 49.2	Safe R	
	D: Detch 24.0	D: Rahall 44.6			

*Indicates an incumbent who has retired or indicated that he or she will not run for re-election in 2018.

Note: The consensus among the experts (see the note at the end of Appendix A) is that these 19 districts are safe for one party or the other. At least one of the experts, however, sees some possibility for change in these 19 districts.

For updates, comments and dialogues please go to www. peopleinpolitics.com.